The
Horror Readers' Advisory

The Librarian's Guide
to Vampires,
Killer Tomatoes,
and Haunted Houses

ALA READERS' ADVISORY SERIES

The Science Fiction and Fantasy Readers' Advisory:
The Librarian's Guide to Cyborgs, Aliens, and Sorcerers

The Mystery Readers' Advisory:
The Librarian's Clues to Murder and Mayhem

The Readers' Advisory Guide to Genre Fiction

The Romance Readers' Advisory:
The Librarian's Guide to Love in the Stacks

The Short Story Readers' Advisory:
A Guide to the Best

THE Horror Readers' Advisory

The Librarian's Guide to Vampires, Killer Tomatoes, and Haunted Houses

Becky Siegel Spratford

Tammy Hennigh Clausen

American Library Association
Chicago   2004

The paper used in this publication meets the minimum requirements of American National Standard for Information Sciences—Permanence of Paper for Printed Library Materials, ANSI Z39.48-1992. ∞

Composition by ALA Editions in Flare Gothic and Berkeley using QuarkXPress 4.1 on a PC platform

Printed on 50-pound white offset, a pH-neutral stock, and bound in 10-point coated cover stock by Victor Graphics

Library of Congress Cataloging-in-Publication Data

Spratford, Becky Siegel
    The horror readers' advisory : the librarian's guide to vampires, killer tomatoes, and haunted houses / Becky Siegel Spratford, Tammy Hennigh Clausen.
       p.   cm. — (ALA readers' advisory series)
    Includes bibliographical references and index.
    ISBN 0-8389-0871-3
    1. Fiction in libraries—United States. 2. Libraries—United States—Special collections—Horror tales. 3. Readers' advisory services—United States. 4. Horror tales—Bibliography. I. Clausen, Tammy Hennigh. II. Title. III. Series.
  Z711.5.S68 2004
  028'.9—dc22   2003025530

Printed in the United States of America.

08 07 06 05 04   5 4 3 2 1

CONTENTS

ACKNOWLEDGMENTS

We have many people to acknowledge, without whom this book would not have been completed. First we need to thank Gail Lofgren, former director of the Berwyn Public Library, for giving two young librarians the chance to create an entire Readers' Advisory Department from scratch; and the current director, Bill Hensley, for trusting us to keep pushing the envelope of traditional library services. We also need to acknowledge the great patrons at the Berwyn Public Library for their patience, support, and enthusiasm. They have learned to trust our professional opinions, even if it meant confusing them by moving the books around umpteen times.

We would also like to acknowledge Marlene Chamberlain and the staff at ALA Editions for trusting us to carry on the well-regarded tradition of the Readers' Advisory Series. We are also extremely lucky to be readers' advisors in northeastern Illinois. This luck of geography has allowed us to work with outstanding readers' advisors as well as have the support of an established network of librarians offering these services. And of course we cannot forget the man who initially got us excited about readers' advisory, Professor Bill Crowley at Dominican University in River Forest, Illinois. Without his course on the subject, neither of us would have gone into this field, and without his faith in our writing skills, we would never have been offered the chance to write this book in the first place. Bill, we cannot thank you enough.

Over the course of writing this book, we came into contact with many horror experts whose knowledge and experience guided us. Alan Ziebarth, the Chicago Public Library's West Branch manager, gave a presentation at the 2002 ILA Annual Conference entitled "Dark Feasts: Building a Core Horror Fiction Collection" and was extremely helpful. Tammy interviewed

ACKNOWLEDGMENTS

Barry Kaufman, proprietor of the House of Monsters in Chicago (http://thehouseofmonsters.com), picking his brain for information about the world of horror films. His vast knowledge and recommendations contributed greatly to this book.

Becky would like to thank her family, specifically her parents for the hundreds of evenings when they found her in bed, asleep on top of a book, and gently removed her glasses and turned out the light. Becky would also like to thank her husband Eric for his encouragement, love, and understanding, always. And finally, her daughter, Samantha, who was born during the writing of this book, for being the very best baby.

Tammy would like to acknowledge Tobes for his encouragement and support as her de facto research assistant. She would also like to thank her husband John for keeping their lives in order while she was locked in the basement writing.

PREFACE

Welcome to the world of horror fiction, where monsters roam the streets, vampires attack at night, ghosts haunt every home, and mayhem is the norm. Readers have been drawn to works of horror for centuries, and as readers' advisors, we become their navigational assistants. In an attempt to help you to steer your horror readers in the right direction, we have created this book. Our goal was to provide librarians with a ready reference resource for horror-related questions. In this pursuit we have provided chapters detailing the history of horror, how to interview your horror patrons, a detailed description of horror resources, tips for developing your library's horror collection, and how to effectively market your horror collection and services. We have also broken down the vast universe of horror books into eleven subgenres. We have provided an introduction to each subgenre's specific characteristics and appeal factors, along with an annotated sampling of suggested titles. These lists are by no means comprehensive, but rather, they should serve as a starting point for both you and your patrons.

We envision this book as both an introduction for readers' advisors who are unsure of how to manage their horror collections or their horror-related inquiries; and as a resource for the more horror-aware librarians to turn to for either ready reference or new ideas. Although this book is meant to be used as a how-to guide for librarians, we tried to keep it from reading like a textbook. We injected our enthusiasm for the subject directly into the text. We hope that by sharing our battle-tested techniques, personal favorites, and professional secrets, we can provide you with a unique reference tool.

When we were first approached to write this book, we were flattered, but also a bit frightened. But since this was going to be a guide to all things terrifying, we figured, what emotion could be more fitting, and we accepted the challenge. We hope you find the final product useful. One final reminder as you go about your day-to-day activities as a readers' advisor: we are so lucky to be paid to read for a living; being able to give other people suggestions about their own reading is simply one of the job's perks.

1

The Evolution of Horror
Literature and Film

I had a connoisseur's . . . appreciation of fear. Fear and I were old bud-
dies, despite my best efforts to the contrary. I knew his whole family, his
older brothers Terror and Panic, his little sister, Nightmare, their charming parents, Chaos and Destruction, and all their cousins, Rage,
Depression, Denial, Guilt, Shame, and the rest of the brood. I had first
made my acquaintance with these enlightening folks in my seventh year,
about twenty seconds before being struck by a car and at the moment I
noticed the proximity of the vehicle to myself and understood that an
unhappy collision was in the cards. —Peter Straub

Horror, like the romance genre, has been slow to gain legitimacy in the
literary arena, partly because horror is evolving and keeps reinventing
itself, but also because it has been the victim of fuzzy and overlapping
genre boundaries. Horror has moved from being a literary element within
the pages of science fiction, serial-killer thriller, and dark fantasy novels to
its own defining genre. Under the umbrella classification of speculative
fiction, we often still find horror partnered with fantasy and science fiction. But there are elements in horror fiction that differentiate it from other
genres. The most prominent of these is the author's intention of provoking

terror. There is a powerful voyeuristic thrill for readers to explore the dark, malevolent side of humanity in an imaginative framework. It is the conceivable wickedness lurking within the reader's own psyche. Horror allows us to face our fears and defeat them, as well as providing an escape from the horrors of real life. It is these macabre literary visions that we horror readers find so intriguing. The appeal of horror literature and film is that we can experience these fears of death, the unknown, or the possibilities of our scariest imaginings at a safe distance, unlike real-life horrors such as child abuse, school shootings, and threats of terrorism. The horror genre can be more than entertainment or distraction. At its best, it can provide a venue for the reader to confront rather than evade the dark horrors that lie waiting under the childhood bed, in the musty corners of the hundred-year-old basement, or behind the eyes of our "not quite right" neighbor gardening at midnight using a foul-smelling compost.

One of the most common errors that readers' advisors fall into when approaching horror readers is the misconception that horror is mostly a reading preference of teenage boys. Librarians need to be reminded that horror literature and film have a long and celebrated history. In fact, some of today's best and most popular authors are writing in this genre: Dean Koontz, Stephen King, Anne Rice, Joyce Carol Oates, and Peter Straub are all mainstream, best-selling authors and appeal to a wide audience; not disturbed people with a perverse inclination for blood and guts, but healthy people from all walks of life.

A Brief History of the Horror Genre

Inspired by a dream, Horace Walpole's *Castle of Otranto* is considered the first gothic novel, and its 1765 publication marks the birth of the horror genre. Horror elements had been present in literature prior to this, of course, but after this date there was an explosion of gothic writings with recurring themes and plot lines characterized by "an emphasis on portraying the terrifying, a common insistence on archaic settings, a prominent use of the supernatural, the presence of highly stereotyped characters and the attempt to deploy and perfect techniques of literary suspense."[1] Emphasizing atmosphere over plot development, the gothic novel became synonymous with excess and exaggeration, portraying the terrors of the haunted house, vampires, werewolves, and soulless monsters unleashed on society. John Polidori wrote one of the first vampire novels, *The Vampyre* (1819), in this style, and Matthew Lewis shocked readers with his tale of rape and torture entitled *The Monk* (1796). Ann Radcliffe's *Mysteries of Udolpho* (1765) was set in the sixteenth century and told the story of the orphaned Emily St. Aubert, who upon her parent's death was made the ward of her aunt, Madame Cheron. The aunt marries a sinister Italian, Count Montoni, who carts Emily off to a dilapidated castle in the Apennines and plots to steal her inheritance. Emily must find the means to escape the villainous Montoni and his terrifying castle. Radcliffe's novel was the best-known and most widely read gothic novel until Mary Shelley's masterpiece *Frankenstein* (1818) was published, marking the end of the gothic period.

The gothic tradition influenced some of our best-known classics such as the Brontë sisters' *Jane Eyre* and *Wuthering Heights,* as well as Jane Austen's *Northanger Abbey.* The gothic influence is seen in later revivals and is especially evident in the writings of nineteenth-century American authors such as Edgar Allan Poe, Nathaniel Hawthorne, and Henry James. Using the short story, Poe in particular contributed to the creation of the dark fantasy tradition. As a precursor of modern psychological writing, he perfected the motifs of death and murderous madness. Walpole, Radcliffe, and Lewis had developed the conventions that were drawn upon and fine-tuned by these nineteenth-century authors. Today we still see novels written in the gothic tradition by Joyce Carol Oates and Anne Rice.

At the close of the nineteenth century, intellectuals of the time were uniquely situated to witness the rise of science and technology, as well as what some perceived to be the social and moral decline of the West. The Enlightenment had brought an increased knowledge of the natural world and a weakening of religious dogmas. People began questioning what happened when you died as well as the existence of God. At the same time, T. H. Huxley was teaching that the development of science had occurred when the human brain had evolved to a certain level of complexity. If wisely used, the marvels of science would allow civilization to reach new heights and humanity would evolve even further. But, he warned, humans had begun as lowly creatures and still had a primitive side to their nature. Motivated by this dark side, people could use science to enslave others and manufacture weapons of destruction. The use of science, for good or evil, and mankind's evolutionary process and primal fears became the central themes that the horror genre was to take up in the twentieth century.

The forerunner novel that explored these ideas was *Frankenstein* (1818), giving us the first mad scientist who attempted to replace the natural order of evolution by stripping away God's divine visage and replacing it with his own. The results were disastrous for Dr. Frankenstein, but we were left with a lasting warning of the consequences of playing God. *The Strange Case of Dr. Jekyll and Mr. Hyde* (1886) by Robert Louis Stevenson delved into the mental health of man, the structure of personality, and the fear that we can unknowingly become our own worse nightmare. The possibility of transforming ourselves only to discover that our alter ego is a monster is truly terrifying. In *The Island of Doctor Moreau,* the grandfather of science fiction, H. G. Wells, warned what the world could expect if it failed to find wisdom to control progress. On the surface, Moreau is a mad scientist, as was the case with Dr. Frankenstein. He heartlessly contorts the shapes of his innocent animal subjects in a blind search for forbidden knowledge. But what he is really doing is far worse. Moreau has set himself up as the divine creator of vivisected creatures who in turn view him as their god. Lastly, Bram Stoker gave us *Dracula* (1897), which became synonymous with the vampire motif. *Dracula* is one of the best-selling novels ever written; it has never been out of print and became the prototype for hundreds of other vampire stories and films.[2] In fact, Dracula is the most frequently portrayed character in horror films, according to the *Guinness Book of World Records.*

The early years of the twentieth century were the golden age of the ghost story.[3] M. R. James set the tone and developed many of the clichés of the ghost story, a subgenre that is still very popular. Authors such as Edgar Allan Poe, Henry James, Edith Wharton, H. G. Wells, Anne Rice, and Stephen King have all experimented with ghost stories, leaving a rich tradition of the haunted.

The major horror writer of the early twentieth century was the eccentric H. P. Lovecraft, who withdrew from most of the world except through correspondences, venturing out only on warm summer nights under the cloak of darkness. Lovecraft influenced a number of other writers with his stories about humans' encounters with ancient beings of horrific and alien appearance who occasionally intrude into our world from other dimensions. These are called the Cthulhu Mythos stories and came out in *Weird*

Tales and other magazines. Lovecraft's works, which include *The Case of Charles Dexter Ward* (1928), *At the Mountains of Madness* (1931), and many short stories, attracted a cult following. August Derleth and Donald Wandrei wrote Cthulhu stories after Lovecraft's death and started Arkham House to publish Lovecraft's stories as well as their own. Throughout the pulp era and beyond, young horror writers tried their hand at employing the Cthulhu theme, including Brian Lumley, Robert Bloch, and Colin Wilson.[4]

Modern horror fiction has been greatly influenced by the motion picture industry, to the extent that since the cinema's infancy, novels and films have shared themes and characters, producing a changed popular view of horror. Lon Chaney Sr. popularized horror on film with the Universal Pictures silent films *Man of a Thousand Faces, Phantom of the Opera,* and *The Hunchback of Notre Dame,* which were made in the melodramatic tradition of the late nineteenth century. During the 1930s and 1940s Universal Pictures produced classic atmospheric horror films based on earlier novels. In 1931 Bela Lugosi played his signature role as *Dracula* and Boris Karloff brought *Frankenstein* to the big screen. Karloff showed his theatrical abilities again in 1932 in the portrayal of Imhotep, a 3,700-year-old Egyptian brought back to life in *The Mummy.* Then in 1941 Universal cast Lon Chaney Jr. with Bela Lugosi in *The Wolf Man,* the definitive werewolf film. The impact these films had on popular perceptions of these monsters invented in novels was enormous. They expanded and added to the original creatures, giving visual images to the classic stories.

In the 1950s, England's Hammer Films studio, on the lowest of budgets, took over the horror movie genre, adding an erotic, sensual element as well as making it more graphically violent. Christopher Lee became the star of a much sexier version of Dracula. Picking up what Hollywood had discarded, Hammer Films brought to the screen or remade *The Mummy, The Curse of Frankenstein, Brides of Dracula,* and dozens of others.

Horror fiction almost died out in the 1940s and 1950s, but the movies brought back the genre, reigniting an interest in horror literature. The 1960s saw an increase in explicit gore with films such as George Romero's *Night of the Living Dead* (1968). The decade also saw retellings of the gothic Poe classics. Starring Vincent Price, Hollywood remade *The Black Cat, The Masque of the Red Death* (1964), and *The Pit and the Pendulum* (1961), to name a few. However, it was a tale of split personality that brought the horror novel back to the mainstream audience in Robert Bloch's *Psycho*

(1959). Alfred Hitchcock's film version of this novel a year later made it famous and also set a new benchmark for horror films. Ira Levin told the story of a young married couple in *Rosemary's Baby* (1967); after they move to New York, the wife becomes impregnated with Satan's spawn. This too was made into a pivotal movie the following year. Following on its coattails, William Peter Blatty wrote *The Exorcist* (1971), whose amazingly influential movie version brought in over $100 million in 1973. The story graphically described the battle over the soul of a young girl taken over by an ancient demon.

The 1970s bring us to the modern horror writers. Stephen King made his debut with *Carrie* (1974), and with his many novels, short stories, nonfiction, and film versions he has thrilled audiences worldwide and become a household name. Anne Rice gave us the vampire Louis Pointe de Luc's confessions in *Interview with the Vampire* (1976) and went on to romance her readers with more vampire and witch stories. Clive Barker intensified the sex and violence in the horror genre with his *Books of Blood* series in the mid-1980s. Barker's novels and short stories fed the growing fascination with slasher films in the 1980s—such as the *Halloween* and *Nightmare on Elm Street* movies—by adding one of his own in the *Hellraiser* films, featuring the terrifying sadomasochist, Pinhead.

Horror has evolved into a best-selling genre by borrowing themes and techniques from the past, as well as by forging into new territory and expanding its boundaries. We are left with a plethora of themes, approaches, and subject matter to choose from. Whether we are looking for what librarian Joyce G. Saricks characterizes as "storyteller," slowly building horror; or "visceral," highly intensified violence that is maintained throughout, we have some great horror fiction to choose from.[5] (See figure 1-1.)

The Gothic Authors

Austen, Jane	Gaskell, Elizabeth	Poe, Edgar Allan
Beckford, William	Hawthorne, Nathaniel	Polidori, John
Brontë, Charlotte	Hoffmann, E. T. A.	Radcliffe, Ann
Brontë, Emily	LeFanu, Joseph Sheridan	Shelley, Mary
Collins, Wilkie	Lewis, Matthew	Walpole, Horace
Dickens, Charles	Melville, Herman	

THE EVOLUTION OF HORROR LITERATURE AND FILM

The Ghost Story Authors

Bierce, Ambrose	James, Henry	Onions, Oliver
Blackwood, Algernon	James, M. R.	Stevenson, Robert Louis
Chambers, Robert W.	Machen, Arthur	Stoker, Bram
Jacobs, W. W.	Mare, Walter de la	Wells, H. G.

The Pulp Era Authors

Benchley, Peter	Dahl, Roald	Lovecraft, H. P.
Birch, A. G.	Derleth, August	March, William
Blatty, William Peter	du Maurier, Daphne	Matheson, Richard
Bleiler, E. F.	Hubbard, L. Ron	Price, E. Hoffman
Bloch, Robert	Jackson, Shirley	Wandrei, Donald
Bradbury, Ray	Leiber, Fritz	Whitehead, Henry S.
Cave, Hugh	Levin, Ira	

Modern Horror Authors

Addison, Linda	Golden, Christopher	Preston, Douglas
Banks, Iain M.	Grant, Charles	Rice, Anne
Barker, Clive	Hamilton, Laurell K.	Saul, John
Braunbeck, Gary	Hopkins, Brian A.	Shirley, John
Brite, Poppy Z.	Huff, Tanya	Simmons, Dan
Cacek, P. D.	Jacob, Charleeack	Slade, Michael
Campbell, Ramsey	Jones, Stephen	Somtow, S. P.
Card, Orson Scott	Ketchum, Jack	Stableford, Brian
Castle, Mort	Kiernan, Caitlin	Straub, Peter
Charnas, Suzy McKee	King, Stephen	Strieber, Whitley
Clegg, Douglas	Koontz, Dean	Thomas, Jeffrey
Collins, Nancy	Lansdale, Joe	Urbancik, John
Cook, Robin	Laymon, Richard	Wiater, Stanley
Crichton, Michael	Little, Bentley	Wilson, F. Paul
de Lint, Charles	Lumley, Brian	Wilson, Gahan
Due, Tanarive	McCammon, Robert	Winter, Douglas
Ellis, Bret Easton	Michaels, Barbara	Yarbro, Chelsea Quinn
Fowler, Christopher	Miller, Rex	
Gaiman, Neil	Newman, Kim	
Garton, Ray	Oates, Joyce Carol	

FIGURE 1-1   Horror Writers

NOTES

The epigraph for this chapter is from the *DarkEcho* interview with Peter Straub, http://www.darkecho.com/darkecho/archives/straub.html.

1. David Puter, *Literature of Terror: The History of Gothic Fiction from 1765 to the Present* (New York: Longman Group, 1996), 1.
2. Stoker's Dracula Organisation, Dublin, http://www.bramstokercentre.org/dracula.htm.
3. Michael Stuprich, ed., *Horror* (San Diego, Calif.: Greenhaven, 2001), 21.
4. Stuprich, *Horror.*
5. Joyce G. Saricks, *The Readers' Advisory Guide to Genre Fiction* (Chicago: American Library Association, 2001), 113.

2

The Readers' Advisory Interview

*Matching Horror Novels
with Readers*

All readers' advisory work begins with the interview. Whether you are actually asking a patron questions about his or her reading habits or you are simply drawing a connection between the currently unavailable book they are looking for and another similar book on the shelf, you are using the same basic principles. You are taking the information given to you by the patron, combining it with your professional knowledge, and shaping it all into the choice of a book to give to a reader. This process of matching readers with books is not a science, however. Every library, and even different readers' advisors, may have their own rules and techniques that work best. Therefore, before we begin to share our tips for interviewing potential horror readers, we first need to explain our personal readers' advisory philosophy.

Objectives of the Readers' Advisor

The overall objective of the readers' advisor is to help facilitate the making of connections between readers and books. Those providing these services first need to subscribe to the philosophy that reading has intrinsic value. This is a commonly held belief as it pertains to children, but once adulthood is reached pleasure reading becomes a luxury, or worse, a distraction from the important tasks of our lives. Readers' advisors are in a perfect position to champion the benefits of lifelong reading and continual learning. To do this, readers' advisors must be able to articulate and rally behind the powerful potential that a story has to produce life-altering changes in readers. The impact a novel can have as a catalyst in shaping our beliefs and value system is a familiar experience for most readers. Readers' advisors also need to approach each patron's inquiry with fairness and respect, without any bias toward their own reading preferences. To assist us in reaching these goals, we apply the readers' advisory motto, "never apologize for your reading tastes." This motto helps to keep us focused on our purpose—serving our readers' needs.

We can incorporate what we know about the habits of readers into our provision of readers' advisory services. We know the different approaches patrons take to their reading; what they are motivated by and what they are looking for are different for each individual. This is because readers are not passive: they bring their own experiences to their reading, and it is not uncommon for the most unsuspecting novel to leave the greatest impact. This holds true for horror specifically, as each reader approaches the genre with different objectives and expectations. Readers' advisory services are subjective and their immediate results are difficult to calculate. There is no one right answer to a reader's request for "a good book," and a broadly read library professional needs to be prepared to offer recommendations.

Horror and Its Appeal

"Horror," it has been written, "is not a genre like mystery or science fiction or the western. It is not a *kind* of fiction meant to be confined to the ghetto of a special shelf in libraries or bookstores. Horror is an emotion."[1] This statement leads us into the heart of the interview process. In order for you to help match a horror book with a potential horror reader, you must first understand why a person would read a horror novel at all. This "why" is commonly referred to as the "appeal" of the work. With nonfiction, readers are normally drawn by the subject of the work; with fiction, however, it is how the author chooses to convey his or her story which is often the most important enjoyment factor—sometimes even more important than the genre itself. The ability to articulate a book's appeal can be a difficult skill to master at first; once learned, however, it almost becomes second nature.[2] In our experience working with horror readers, we have found that there are seven appeal factors inherent in the genre which commonly explain why people enjoy the world of the macabre. (See figure 2-1.)

Although each book has its own "feel," horror as a genre does have its own unique appeal factors, the first of which may be the least unique. Although decidedly its own genre, horror can blur over into the boundaries of fantasy. As a result, much of what is appealing about fantasy can be transferred to horror. For example, like fantasy, horror tends to be filled with action, but the stories themselves are character driven. It is the character's quest and growth which are central to the novel's conflict and resolution. This can cause problems when you are recommending horror to a patron who likes adventure stories, which tend to delve less into the psyches of the characters than your average horror novel. Fantasy and horror are also dependent upon the reader's willingness to suspend their disbelief. It is this escape factor that appeals to many horror readers. These similarities being noted, it is also important to point out that not all fantasy readers

---

The following is a quick rundown of the general appeal factors of horror. While each of these points is elaborated upon in the text, this list is a great "cheat sheet" to use as you discuss horror with a patron.

- has similarities with fantasy
- provokes terror
- atmosphere takes center stage over plot development
- allows safe exploration of the dark side of humanity
- gives readers a place where they can face their own fears
- provides an escape from the horrors of real life
- validates belief in the supernatural

FIGURE 2-1   Basic Horror Appeal Factors

will enjoy horror or vice versa. Horror showcases fantasy's darker aspects, yet many fantasy readers like their novels to be lighter romps through a magical land.

Horror may blend at its edges into fantasy, but it also has elements that are wholly its own. It is the combination of these elements that gets to the heart of why people read horror. The most recognizable element is the author's intention of provoking terror. More than any other kind of literature, the horror novel's ultimate objective is to scare by manipulating the reader's emotions. It gives a voice to our fears, inspiring dark emotions of panic, chaos, destruction, aversion and disgust. The author can be less concerned with logic or realism than with the need to create a squeamish uneasiness. Often the subtlest and most terrifying moments are achieved through suggestion rather than through shocking scenes and brutality. Atmosphere is very important in achieving this. More important than the actual plot development, we need to *feel* the worlds that may have beings we know do not exist. To this end horror goes after a visceral response in the reader, attacking him or her in the gut. A horror novel creates a fear we can palpably feel with all five of our senses. It is important to note, however, that in order to evoke this fear, horror authors sometimes use graphic depictions of violence and sex.

A good horror novel is written in a way that frightens us but keeps us from hiding under the bed by coaxing us to continue reading. A reader of horror may enjoy the shock inherent in these works, but it takes more than the obvious "fear factor" to keep the horror reader coming back for more. One of the most compelling aspects of the genre is its focus on the dark side of human nature. If you doubt that human beings feel an intrinsic interest in evil, we remind you of the numerous movies and television shows that focus on heinous crimes, the 24-hour news coverage of appalling tragedies, and, of course, the millions of books sold by Stephen King himself. Many people are instinctively drawn to explore the malevolent side of humanity, and horror novels are a way to do this safely. Yes, some people are seduced by evil thoughts enough to commit horrid acts; however, for the vast majority of humanity, horror novels are simply a safe way to acknowledge the wickedness within their own psyches and take a small peek into this illicit world.

Horror also allows readers to face their own fears. We are all scared of something, and reading a story of others overcoming monsters, witches, or curses empowers us to face the horrors in our own lives. As bad as our worst fear may be, it cannot be worse than staring down a thousand-year-old golem. Conversely, horror is a great escape from the real horrors of life. Fiction often enables the reader to escape the real world, but horror specifically seems to be a popular antidote to hard times. As Stephen King himself has noted, "Horror movies and horror novels have always been popular, but every 10 to 20 years they seem to enjoy a cycle of increased popularity and visibility. These periods almost always seem to coincide with periods of fairly serious economic and/or political strain."[3] The economy may be in the tank, but it is easy to forget about your finances while you are engrossed in a struggle between good and evil in the pages of a novel.

The final appeal factor which we have found draws readers to horror is the genre's ability to validate the reader's belief in the supernatural. The recent surge in popularity of psychic telephone hotlines and television programs, coupled with a long-standing interest in the "occult" section of the nonfiction shelves at most public libraries, stand as a testament to our interest in the supernatural. Horror feeds off this natural curiosity by creating situations in which unexplainable phenomena and unearthly creatures are the norm. Everyday life can be a series of mechanical and logical events, but many people become bored by this predictability and look for more. Still others are looking for answers or explanations to the problems and tragedies in their lives. For these reasons and others, the supernatural becomes an alluring solution. One of the most common supernatural events which the genre tackles is the issue of life after death. Ghosts, spirits, zombies, vampires, and mummies all come back from the dead in some fashion. Even though these life-after-death scenarios usually involve the risen being or spirit wreaking havoc on living characters in the novel, it is oddly comforting to the reader to have his or her fears about what happens to us after we die answered in some way. Yes, we would rather ghosts and spirits be of the friendly sort, but it is reassuring to see the existence of life after death, even if it is in the pages of a horror novel.

We by no means proclaim that every horror book combines all of these appeal factors; in fact, these are only general characteristics that help to create the emotion of horror. Different subgenres within horror will rely on, and even develop further, a specific appeal factor or two. In our chapters on the horror subgenres, we point out the appeal factors and characteristics that set each subgenre apart from the others.

Also keep in mind that each individual work will have its own specific appeal factors as they pertain to specific story and author, such as a fast or slow pace, a linear or disjointed plot line, and an open or closed ending, just to name a few. These more generalized appeal factors also need to be considered because they do play a part in the reader's enjoyment of a novel, depending on his or her preferences. To help untangle this appeal mess, especially if you are not a big horror reader yourself, we suggest reading *Stephen King's Danse Macabre,* a nonfiction work that is part social scientific analysis of the genre and part personal memoir of King's love for works of horror. What better way could there be to get to the heart of why people read horror than to hear why this master loves it so much? King has been able to tap into the most appealing aspects of the genre, drawing millions of readers into the fantastic stories he creates. One of King's most memorable comments about horror comes quite early in this book: "the work of horror really is a dance—a moving rhythmic search. And what it's looking for is the place where you, the viewer or the reader, live at your most primitive level."[4] Just a cursory perusal of *Danse Macabre* can get even the most timid librarian excited about horror.

The Interview

In any situation where you are recommending a book to a reader, you are actively involved in the interview process. For many librarians, "the interview" has become so much second nature that they may not even be aware it is happening. But it is important, even for the most seasoned veteran, to take a step back and dissect the process. With horror specifically, there are two distinct types of interviews that you will be engaged in. The first, and more obvious, is the questions you must ask the reader who is explicitly seeking a horror novel. The second, and more subtle, is the questions you will focus on when you suspect a patron may enjoy a work of horror even though that is not what is being specifically requested. In either instance, the key to doing our job successfully is to get the patron talking about books; specifically, books he or she has enjoyed recently, authors they can't get enough of, and types of novels they tend to enjoy. Sometimes a patron can resist your advances, but armed with the right questions and perseverance, you should be able to get just enough information out of the patron to work your professional magic.

Let us begin with the more obvious interview situation: the patron who is requesting a horror novel. This request can come in many forms, including requests for something to read when the new Stephen King book is out, queries about new or different horror authors, or inquiries about specific horror subgenres. No matter how the specifics change, all of these questions are examples in which a patron is seeking a horror work. How well you can help these patrons will be based on how well you approach the interview process. First, you need to engage the horror-seeking patron in casual conversation about his or her likes and dislikes in the genre. Who are their favorite authors? What are their favorite horror books? And most importantly, you should ask the patron what they like most about these works or authors. It cannot be stressed enough that what is "appealing" about an author or work is the most important clue in our search for a reading suggestion.

In these beginning moments of the interview process, it is important for you to put the patron at ease, especially if he or she is not forthcoming in answering your questions. Make this a conversation, not an inquest. When the patron answers one question, do not simply fire back the next question on your list. Rather, you should respond to her in some way. For example, when asked why she likes Stephen King, your patron may respond that although the creepy factor in his work is great, she most enjoys the fact that he is a good storyteller first and foremost. To this, you can either recount why you like Stephen King, or if you do not particularly enjoy him, you could instead talk about how important it is for any author to be a good storyteller. Whatever you end up saying to the patron, you should make an effort to have a conversation with her. Not only will it make the patron more willing to divulge information that can help you do your job, but also it puts you both at ease.

Let's continue with this same example as we move further into the interview process. Now that you are conversing about King, storytelling, and horror, it is time to ask a few key questions. You should ask all of your horror readers how they feel about violence, gore, and sex in their stories. Works of horror run the gamut from the extremely tame to the deliberate gross-out. Understanding your patron's taste for graphic descriptions can save you from making a disastrous suggestion. You should also try to find out if there is a particular subgenre the patron enjoys. This can also be crucial. Take Anne Rice readers, for instance. We have found that many of them hate her non-vampire stories and will only read other works of horror if they include a vampire or two. In this case, you should not waste too much time trying to locate a book outside of this subgenre.

In our example, we can assume our King reader can stomach books with a fair amount of blood, guts, and sexual situations, but these aspects should not be the focus of the story. We can also assume that our patron would read a horror book from just about any subgenre as long as it was a well-told tale. Of course, in a real interview situation you would be making these assumptions in your head or jotting them down while you were conversing with the patron, and then verifying them by directly asking the patron if she thought those were fair assumptions. At this point you should begin suggesting authors or specific books. This situation calls for the suggestion of a work by Robert McCammon, Dean Koontz, or Orson Scott Card. All three are wonderful storytellers who write compelling novels that cross the lines between horror subgenres and even into other genres.

We use Stephen King as our example here because it is one of the most common horror-related questions we receive. However, you can follow the general advice here to help you match any horror reader with a new book. Just remember that you will not always be able to give the patron a suggestion right away, especially if you are less familiar with horror. Politely ask him or her to give you a phone number or have them return at a later time so that you may have some time to use this book and other professional resources to come up with the best suggestion. But if you do make the patron wait, we suggest that you provide a list of five to ten authors or books as proof of the time you needed to complete the task, and as a thank-you for his or her patience.

Now we need to move on to the second, more subtle type of horror interview, matching a non-horror reader with a tale of terror. This scenario gets to the heart of what we do as readers' advisors. Any librarian armed with the NoveList database can take the title of a book enjoyed by the patron and spit back a list of "similar works." However, only the trained readers' advisor can help readers match their unique reading interests with the wide variety of materials available. While it is clear that part of our job is to help patrons find exactly what they are looking for, it is just as important for us to point out works which they might not have found if left to their own devices. For instance, we have many murder mystery readers at our library. They come in at least once a week and take out an armload of books. Inevitably, once a month, one of these readers will approach our desk to complain that he or she has "read everything" we have. Of course this is not true; the patron has simply run out of known reading options. Situations such as these provide a perfect opportunity to introduce the patron to an entirely new universe of materials. Sometimes we forget about this part of our job as readers' advisors. We are our patrons' guide to the thousands of titles at their fingertips, and they expect us to steer them to places they would not have thought to explore on their own. With mystery, fantasy, and thriller readers especially, horror may be a good option, but you need to do some investigating first. We have devised a checklist to help you make this determination. (See figure 2-2.) The four points on this list represent the most crucial appeal factors of most horror works. If the patron is averse to more than one of these, you should be very careful before steering him toward horror. However, by using some of the tips from the horror reader interview above, a conversation with your mystery buff might end with him going home with a Ramsey Campbell book under his arm.

If you have a patron who is looking for new authors because he or she has "read everything you have here," the best course of action is to try to move them into an unfamiliar genre of writers. To see if a patron is a good candidate for introduction to the world of the macabre, use this checklist as a guide. Generally, we have found that at least three checks denotes a reader who would enjoy most mainstream horror. With only two checks, we recommend still trying a horror novel, but the choice will require you to do a little research in order to suggest the correct book. One check, and we suggest looking to another genre to expand your patron's reading horizons.

☐ Patron enjoys thrillers of any kind

☐ Patron does not mind blood and guts

☐ Patron prefers character-driven plots to action-driven stories

☐ Patron does not mind fantasy elements in their novels

FIGURE 2-2 Checklist of Appeal Factors to Lead a Non-Horror Reader to the Genre

Conclusion

Interviewing patrons is how we as readers' advisors are able to best help the individual reader. Each reader enjoys a book for his or her own reasons, and two people who love the same book may note completely different factors in that work which they find the most appealing. We need to use the patron's own words to find another book he or she may enjoy. However, it also helps if we are aware of the key appeal factors within the major genres. As we discussed with horror, understanding what people find appealing about a genre ahead of time will help you to steer the interview, and ultimately, will allow you to be better at your job. But remember not to be afraid to mention horror to the non-horror reader. Librarians sometimes need to be reminded of horror's rich history and mass appeal. The dozens of holds at your library for the latest Anne Rice or Stephen King novel are a testament to the genre's appeal to a wide audience.

NOTES

1. Douglas E. Winter, ed., *Prime Evil: New Stories by the Masters of Modern Horror* (New York: New American Library, 1988).
2. If this concept is new to you, we recommend reading chapter 3 of Joyce Saricks and Nancy Brown's seminal work, *Readers' Advisory Service in the Public Library* (Chicago: American Library Association, 1997).
3. Stephen King, *Stephen King's Danse Macabre* (New York: Everest House, 1981), 40.
4. King, *Danse Macabre,* 17–18.

3

The Classics

*Time-Tested Tales
of Terror*

Making lists of "classic" books is about as clichéd as a readers' advisor can get. Nonetheless, we still advocate the exercise of identifying "the classics" within the horror genre because, while these books may fit into other subgenres, as classics, they have distinct characteristics and appeal factors. Unfortunately, elevating works to this subgenre can be messy. Simply by creating this list we are forced to put ourselves on the line and scrounge up enough hubris to actually identify the canon of horror literature. In an attempt to legitimize our take on the classics, we have set up two qualifications for a work to make the list. The first is a simple time limit: to make our list, each work must have been published before 1974. Why 1974? We are assuming a book must be at least thirty years old to have earned the right to be considered a "classic," but 1974 was also the year Stephen King published his first book, *Carrie*. Since the appearance of King and his enormous popularity marked a turning point in the genre, we have decided that all of the classics on our list must come from the pre-King era. Our second qualification is a bit more subjective. Since not every major work of horror fiction published before 1974 could be on our list, we used a combination of sources, including the 14th edition of *The Fiction Catalog* (H. W. Wilson), Fonseca and Pulliam's *Hooked on Horror*, and Jones and Newman's *Horror: The Best 100 Books* and added a pinch of our own judgment to whittle the list down to the twenty-two most representative works. We carefully chose these books for both their historical significance and their readability. We understand that by setting the characteristics of a classic ourselves, the following list may leave out a few well-known horror books, maybe even your personal favorite, but we think that the list provided here stands as a strong representation of the history of horror literature.

"The Classics" is the only artificially created subgenre in this work. Most books naturally separate themselves by the nature of their subject matter, but these works have been elevated to the canon by virtue of their publication dates and historical importance. While their subjects range from haunted houses to vampires to demonic possession, encompassing almost every subgenre along the way, it is still possible to identify the unique appeal factors that would make these books of interest to your patrons. First, the classics appeal to all readers for the respect they carry. Works like Mary Shelley's *Frankenstein,* Henry James's *The Turn of the Screw,* and Emily Brontë's *Wuthering Heights* are often mentioned as part of the canon of great Western literature. Many readers, no matter what their genre(s) of preference, are drawn to classic literature; these patrons would be the perfect audience for this list.

Second, "the classics" provide non-horror reading patrons with a perfect introduction to a whole new genre of literature. Those horror books defined as classics have two specific appeal factors which make them the perfect introduction for new horror readers: they tend to be tamer than today's tales, both in violence and sexual content, and most of them (or their authors) will already be somewhat familiar to your patrons. As a result, this subgenre serves as the perfect springboard to horror for the novice. Remember, it is our job as readers' advisors to connect readers with books, especially those in genres they have not explored on their own. People tend to be creatures of habit; thus, your typical mystery readers may not venture beyond that section. However, when those same patrons proclaim that they have "already read everything here," why not introduce them to horror by recommending Arthur Conan Doyle's familiar collection *Tales of Terror and Mystery?* We don't advocate that you try to thrust horror books onto unsuspecting patrons, but you should always be trying to give your readers new experiences, and the classics provide the perfect opportunity to introduce, for example, suspense lovers to Edgar Allan Poe.

Finally, although horror is a vast genre, and it is impossible to expect readers of one subgenre to find another just as appealing, the classics are all well-written and engaging books, which are sure to put a wide audience under their spell. Most readers' advisors keep a list of "Best Bets" or "Good Reads" around for the inevitable patron who comes in and wants you to choose a good book for them. Three books from this subgenre, Daphne du Maurier's *Rebecca,* Shirley Jackson's *The Haunting of Hill House,* and H. G. Wells's *The Invisible Man* all sit in our "Good Reads" file, and they have yet to disappoint. So whether you are trying to find something different for a patron who feels stuck in a rut, need a book for a-tried-and-true horror fan, or are just looking for a good read, you will find this list of the classics to be the most versatile and useful of the horror subgenre lists in your daily work as a readers' advisor.

Bradbury, Ray. *Something Wicked This Way Comes.* 1962.

> When a carnival comes into a small Illinois town a week before Halloween, two adolescent boys are forever changed by its secrets, mysteries, and horrors.

Brontë, Emily. *Wuthering Heights.* 1847.

> Driven mad by his thwarted love, Heathcliff seeks to destroy the Linton and Earnshaw families after the death of his beloved, Catherine. Revenge, however, cannot calm the deluded Heathcliff, who is forever haunted by Catherine's ghost at Wuthering Heights.

Conrad, Joseph. *The Heart of Darkness.* 1902.

> The true horrors of imperialism are exposed in this haunting short novel as Marlowe, an experienced explorer, tells of his journey in search of the white trader, Kurtz, deep inside the African continent.

Doyle, Arthur Conan. *Tales of Terror and Mystery.* 1977.

> With an introduction by Nina Conan Doyle, Doyle's daughter, this collection is split into two sections: Terror and Mystery. The "tales of terror" include "The Horror of the Heights," "The Leather Funnel," "The New Catacomb," "The Case of Lady Sannox," "The Terror of Blue John Gap," and "The Brazilian Cat."

du Maurier, Daphne. *Rebecca.* 1938.

> Mrs. de Winter may be a new bride, but she is not the first Mrs. de Winter; the deceased Rebecca held that honor previously. Although

she is physically dead, Rebecca is still very much a force for the new Mrs. de Winter to contend with.

Hawthorne, Nathaniel. *The House of the Seven Gables.* 1851.

The Pynchons of Salem, Massachusetts, may be one of the most distinguished families in town, but they are also held victim to a centuries-old curse. Hawthorne based this novel on a curse placed upon his own family by a woman whom they had sent to her death during the Salem witch trials.

Hitchcock, Alfred, ed. *Alfred Hitchcock Presents: Stories Not for the Nervous.* 1965.

This classic short story collection was handpicked and edited by the master of fear and suspense and contains more than twenty terrifying tales. Authors of note include Ray Bradbury, Dorothy Sayers, and Richard Matheson. A sequel, *Alfred Hitchcock Presents: More Stories Not for the Nervous,* is shorter and is also worth a read.

Irving, Washington. "The Legend of Sleepy Hollow." 1819–20.

This is a tale about love and a headless horseman in the eighteenth century. Ichabod Crane, a schoolteacher, moves from Connecticut to Sleepy Hollow, New York, where he falls in love and learns the truth behind the myth of the headless horseman stalking the town.

Jackson, Shirley. *The Haunting of Hill House.* 1959.

In this horror classic, four different people come together for a stay at the notorious Hill House. What transpires in this eerie mansion is both physically and emotionally terrifying.

James, Henry. *The Turn of the Screw.* 1898.

Two small children on their uncle's estate are put in the care of a young governess. Everything is going well until the uncle's servant and the previous governess return from the dead to collect the souls of the children.

LeFanu, Joseph Sheridan. *Carmilla.* 1872.

Predating *Dracula* by twenty-five years, *Carmilla* is a gothic story about the relationship between a female vampire, Carmilla, and her innocent friend, the unnamed narrator. *Carmilla* has been the acknowledged inspiration for over a dozen vampire films.

Levin, Ira. *Rosemary's Baby.* 1967.

In this chilling tale, a young woman is impregnated with Satan's spawn. This work, which was made into a well-known film, masterfully blends fantasy and reality.

Lewis, Matthew. *The Monk.* 1796.

This novel follows the popular Madrid monk, Ambrosio, who is hiding a huge secret: his love for the beautiful Matilda. When his lust overcomes him, Ambrosio rapes her, and is condemned to death for his actions. But it is when the monk sells his soul to the Devil in exchange for his life that this tale really gets interesting. Republished in 2002 with an introduction by Stephen King.

Lovecraft, H. P. *The Best of H.P. Lovecraft: Bloodcurdling Tales of Horror and the Macabre.* 1982.

Publishing short stories mainly in pulp magazines, Lovecraft was largely unknown during his life. However, he has since become a cult figure in the horror community. He is best known for his Cthulhu Mythos stories, which take place in the imaginary town of Arkham (based on his hometown of Providence, Rhode Island). This book collects sixteen of Lovecraft's best stories. A must read for any horror lover.

March, William. *The Bad Seed.* 1954.

Amidst the "happy" homes of suburbia, evil lurks in the form of a seemingly sweet and innocent young girl, Rhoda Penmark. Rhoda will kill if she does not get her way. What can her family do to stop the serial killer they have spawned? March is credited with creating the original "evil child" tale which has since been imitated dozens of times in print, television, and film.

Maupassant, Guy de. *The Dark Side of Guy de Maupassant.* 1989.

Maupassant is often called France's greatest short story writer, and this collection of his horror writings delves into the supernatural. Scholars have stated that many of these stories also parallel the author's own descent into madness.

Poe, Edgar Allan. *The Collected Tales of Edgar Allan Poe.* 1992.

There are many collections of Poe's tales, and any will do. Poe's stories thrill and chill even today. He is the master of psychological horror. These stories will appeal to almost any reader.

Shelley, Mary. *Frankenstein.* 1818.

Often cited as the first horror novel ever written, *Frankenstein* is the story of a scientist's effort to create life. Shelley uses her novel to describe the horrors humankind can expect to confront when it foolishly tries to conquer nature.

Stevenson, Robert Louis. *The Strange Case of Dr. Jekyll and Mr. Hyde.* 1886.

In nineteenth-century London, Dr. Jekyll performs an experiment in which he attempts to separate his pure, good side from his dark, evil qualities. He succeeds and splits his personality in two, but his other half is the evil Mr. Hyde.

Stoker, Bram. *Dracula.* 1897.

This is the most familiar of the vampire tales. Count Dracula hides during the day, but from dusk to dawn has the strength of twenty men, can summon armies of rats and wolves, and, oh yes, he seeks victims from which he can suck their blood.

Walpole, Horace. *The Castle of Otranto.* 1765.

In this gothic romance, Conrad, the heir to Otranto, is mysteriously ill. In order to keep their family dynasty intact, Conrad's father plans to take his son's place at the wedding altar. That is, until supernatural forces get in the way. *The Castle of Otranto* is a fine example of the gothic novels which stand as precursors to the true horror novel.

Wells, H. G. *The Invisible Man.* 1897.

A stranger covered in bandages comes to the small English town of Iping. He has discovered the secret of making himself invisible, but he soon finds that invisibility makes his life harder. After committing a murder, he becomes the victim of a manhunt.

4

Ghosts and Haunted Houses

Home Scream Home

Many a child has been introduced to the horror genre with a ghost story. Think back to your own childhood, for example: ghost stories told around the campfire, hearing about the neighborhood haunted house, and if you're a bit younger, reading the hugely popular *Goosebumps* books. Psychologists have noted this phenomenon over the years, and it has now become accepted belief that as we enter late childhood we begin to understand that all things eventually die, including ourselves. We then spend the rest of our lives coming to terms with our own mortality. The ghost story, and its implicit message of life after death, is in a sense comforting. We hear, read, and see films of ghost stories from a very early age; in fact, the ghost story is the most common experience people have with horror fiction. So it should come as no surprise that ghosts and their hauntings have emerged as one of the most pervasive themes in the horror novel throughout its history.

Horror fiction as we know it today began with the gothic ghost story. Novels like Horace Walpole's 1765 classic *The Castle of Otranto,* and the incomparable *Wuthering Heights* (1847) by Emily Brontë are among numerous examples of this rich tradition. In these works, old mansions that have been witness to terrible events meet troubled people. The end result involves a dollop of haunting, a healthy serving of ghosts, and generally a dash of romance for extra appeal. The ghost story evolved like other types of literature, and by the end of the nineteenth century works like Henry James's *The Turn of the Screw* had become much more psychological in nature. The ghosts began to reflect the inner feelings of the haunted party, his guilt, remorse, or paranoia. In the late twentieth and early twenty-first centuries the ghost story has remained relevant and fresh. In fact, some of today's most popular horror writers such as Stephen King, Anne Rice, and Peter Straub have all written noteworthy books within this subgenre, and recent works like Thomas Tessier's *Fog Heart* have won prestigious awards.

Even though the ghost story has been around for centuries, there are basic characteristics your readers can expect from all works within this subgenre. The general question that must be addressed and resolved in every ghost story is why the spirits of the dead cannot rest. Characters who encounter ghosts generally enter a new environment, such as in John Saul's *Nathaniel*, or try to make peace with a person or a place to which something terrible has happened, as in Poppy Z. Brite's *Drawing Blood*. With this change of situation comes a confrontation with at least one ghost. Whether the spirit is malevolent or not, the characters in these novels cannot rest until the motivation behind the haunting is understood. Usually, at this point, the characters can either help the ghost obtain what he or she needs to rest, or, if necessary, use the knowledge gained to defeat the spirit.

This leads us to the second characteristic of the ghost story. The ghost sightings themselves are generally a reflection of the complex internal feelings of the person seeing the spirits. Guilt is the most common of these feelings. Peter Straub's *Ghost Story* is a good example of this phenomenon. In this novel, four old men are at the center of strange events in their quiet town. These events force them to come to terms with their part in the death of a young woman decades before. Generally, the haunted must deal with a ghost who is the personification of the guilt or remorse they have been holding inside themselves. This extra psychological dimension adds depth to the ghost story. It allows for the creation of a complex and interesting protagonist whose struggle becomes even more compelling as he is forced to battle both the supernatural and his own self.

The appeal of the ghost story is easy to comprehend. Beyond the intriguing self versus supernatural and self versus self conflicts that rule most of these works, the novels also affirm our tendency to believe in life after death. Although most people don't want to be forced to roam the halls of someone else's home for the rest of eternity, reading about these hauntings reassures us that something happens to our spirit after our body ceases to live. It is less frightening to think about living in a haunted house than it is to confront our own mortality.

Ghost stories also play on the universal human fear of "things that go bump in the night." This subgenre is dominated by dark corners, old creaky houses, terrible tragedies, and untimely deaths. The spectres that appear when the lights go out are not for the faint of heart. Humans may have conquered the dark thousands of years ago, but ever since that first spark of fire illuminated the night, we have remained frightened of the shadows. The ghost story (like vampire and werewolf tales) is dependent upon darkness; the hauntings most often occur where light is dim, so that the haunted can never be absolutely sure of what they just witnessed.

Finally, because these works appeal to some of our basic human fears, are fueled by compelling internal conflicts, and have been a part of our storytelling tradition from childhood on, it should come as no surprise that the novels in this subgenre cover a wide range of subjects. There is a ghost story tailored to just about every reader. For those who enjoy romance, there are numerous works by Barbara Erskine and Barbara Michaels. If it is a detective story your reader craves, they could try James Herbert's *Haunted* or Noel Hynd's *A Room for the Dead*. There are even ghost tales with elements of science fiction and fantasy, like William Hope Hodgson's *The House on the Borderland*. Thus, as a readers' advisor you can be confident there is a ghost story for each of your readers, and hopefully our short list can help you begin to sort out the numerous offerings within this popular subgenre.

Anson, Jay. *The Amityville Horror.* 1977.

> The Lutz family moves into their new home on Amityville, Long Island, knowing that it has already been the site of a mass murder. Despite this knowledge, they are not prepared for the strange things that begin to happen around them.

Bloch, Robert. *Lori.* 1989.

> Lori returns from college to find her home burning with her parents trapped inside. After this tragedy Lori discovers her odd connection to a mysterious stranger, Priscilla Fairmount, faces terrifying nightmares, and hears ghosts calling to her.

Brite, Poppy Z. *Drawing Blood.* 1993.

> See chapter 13, "Splatterpunk."

Brontë, Emily. *Wuthering Heights.* 1847.

> See chapter 3, "The Classics."

Campbell, Ramsey. *Nazareth Hill.* 1997.

> As a young child, Amy sees a ghost through the window of Nazarill, a run-down building. Eight years later, after Amy's father becomes the caretaker of the now-renovated building, an older tenant dies. Before it is too late, Amy must convince everyone that his death is the work of a ghost out for revenge.

Card, Orson Scott. *Homebody.* 1998.

> Architect Don Lark has turned to buying and fixing up old homes after the tragic death of his daughter. His newest acquisition comes with a mysterious tunnel, a female squatter, and very odd neighbors. Card, a popular writer in all genres of speculative fiction, takes on Lark's story and ultimately uses it to illustrate how love can overcome evil.

Erskine, Barbara. *House of Echoes.* 1996.

> Jocelyn Grant moves into her recently inherited Essex Manor with her son and husband. But when it becomes apparent that the home is haunted by an evil presence that only threatens the male members of the family, Jocelyn must confront the ghost in order to save her family. Also try Erskine's *Midnight Is a Lonely Place* (1995).

Herbert, James. *Haunted.* 1990.

> David Ash has made his living as a psychic investigator debunking false claims of supernatural activity. But when the Mariell family hire him to hopefully prove wrong their own suspicions about their haunted country home, Ash may have finally come face-to-face with the real thing. This book does not disappoint.

Hodgson, William Hope. *The House on the Borderland.* 1908.

> In the Irish countryside a diary is found at a deteriorating country estate. In it an elderly man has recounted his descent into a pit under his home, his battles with piglike creatures, and his traveling through

time. With elements of fantasy, science fiction, and horror, this novel was the inspiration for future works by H. P. Lovecraft.

Hynd, Noel. *A Room for the Dead.* 1994.

In this blend of both horror and mystery, detective Frank O'Hara is on the brink of retirement when a gruesome murder is committed. The crime appears to be the work of the notorious serial killer Gary Ledbetter, but Frank was a key player in the capture and execution of Ledbetter years earlier. How can Frank catch a ghost?

Jackson, Shirley. *The Haunting of Hill House.* 1959.

See chapter 3, "The Classics."

James, Henry. *The Turn of the Screw.* 1898.

See chapter 3, "The Classics."

Kahn, James. *Poltergeist.* 1982.

Although many readers will be familiar with the movie, *Poltergeist* is just as compelling in written form. The Freelings' home is built on top of a burial ground, and the disturbed spirits are not too happy about it. The ghosts begin to make their presence known by contacting six-year-old Carol Anne Freeling through the family's television set.

King, Stephen. *The Shining.* 1977.

Jack Torrance brings his family along on his new job as the winter caretaker of the Overlook Hotel in Colorado. In true King fashion, we find that this is not your ordinary hotel, as it is haunted by spirits which are trying to overtake the family. *The Shining* is both a quintessential haunted house story and one of King's best novels. *The Tommyknockers* (1987) and *Bag of Bones* (1998) also fit into this subgenre.

Masterton, Graham. *The House That Jack Built.* 1996.

Craig and Effie Bellman purchase Valhalla, a New Orleans mansion with a terrible past. While working to restore it, Craig becomes absorbed in the house and its evil history, but will he meet with the same untimely death as each of Valhalla's past owners?

Matheson, Richard. *Hell House*. 1977.

This book was written in homage to Shirley Jackson's *The Haunting of Hill House* and was also a credited influence on Stephen King's *The Shining. Hell House* is the story of a legendary haunted home known as Belasco House. Curious people have tried to explore Belasco House and discover it secrets, but all previous trips have resulted in disaster. Now four strangers will try to unlock the mystery behind this most haunted of houses.

McCammon, Robert. *The Night Boat*. 1980.

After decades hidden in the ocean's depths, a Nazi submarine surfaces. Thinking they are helping to preserve an important piece of history, the townspeople tow it to shore. Unfortunately, inside this ship the entire Nazi crew is mummified but still alive due to a voodoo curse, setting off a haunting of horrifying proportions.

Michaels, Barbara. *House of Many Shadows*. 1974.

Meg may be recuperating from a head injury, but she is clear-headed enough to understand that something strange is going on in the old home she inherited from her cousin. When the caretaker, Andy, also begins to witness horrifying visions, Meg's terrifying suspicions are validated. Barbara Michaels again showcases her proven blend of horror and romance in this book. Also try *The Crying Child* (1971).

Rice, Anne. *Violin*. 1997.

The master of the vampire tale proves she can hold her own with this time-bending ghost tale. Trianna is mourning many losses, and the only thing that seems to lift her spirits is the beautiful violin music played by a ghost, Stephan. Stephan takes Trianna on a tormenting journey, ultimately forcing her to confront her depression and her life in general. Although this book does not have vampires in it, the author's fans will recognize the writing style, setting, and emotions found within any Rice book.

Rickman, Phil. *December*. 1994.

The twelfth-century ruins of "The Abbey" hold many dark secrets. When a rock band called The Philosopher's Stone chooses to record their first album there, the secrets begin to surface, resulting in the death of a band member. In an attempt to end the horrors, the group agrees to disband and destroy their tapes. But thirteen years later the tapes resurface, and the bandmates must reunite and confront the evil.

Saul, John. *Nathaniel.* 1984.

When her husband Mark dies, Janet and her son Michael return to Mark's hometown for the funeral. There Janet finds a farm she never knew Mark owned, and Michael discovers the town's secret, a boy named Nathaniel who has haunted the community for over a century. Also try in this genre *The Blackstone Chronicles* (1997) and *When the Wind Blows* (1990).

Straub, Peter. *Ghost Story.* 1979.

After an elderly man, Edward Wanderley, dies, strange things start happening in the small town of Milburn, New York. The events force his four friends to come face-to-face with a tragic event from their past. This is the least traditional ghost story on the list, but it is a seminal work by an important author.

Tessier, Thomas. *Fog Heart.* 1998.

Two couples trying to understand the ghosts who are visiting them separately consult Oona, a psychic. Thinking their experiences are somehow connected, Oona introduces the two couples and conducts their séances together. This is a story as much about the relationships between the living as it is about the ghosts with whom they are trying to communicate.

Walpole, Horace. *The Castle of Otranto.* 1765.

See chapter 3, "The Classics."

5

Mummies, Zombies, and Golems

*The Walking Dead
under Wraps*

That is why so often there is within us this unconscious understanding that we—and the scientist-archaeologist on our behalf—should not tamper with things that are gone. It is a fact of superstition, but it still governs the way we think. —Seth Holt

At the close of the nineteenth century, philosophers and thinkers stood at a moral crossroad in regard to emerging industrialization and the marvels of science. H. G. Wells and his contemporaries were experimenting with the idea that humanity was destined either to progress or decline, depending on the direction in which man chose to use the inventions of science. It was this use of science for good or evil, and humanity's evolutionary processes, that later became the central themes of fiction involving monsters. Advanced technology proves to be malevolent and terrifying, and liberates the forbidden dark side of humanity as epitomized in monsters.

Mummies, zombies, and golems are undead beings who are capable of great evil. Their undead qualities are reminiscent of vampire legends, while their reanimation invariably recalls Frankenstein's story. These stories not only call into question the role of science, but also man's disregard for religious and cultural norms. Lacking souls, these creatures are set apart from other monsters by the magic, ancient myths, and cultural traditions on which they are based. Zombies from Haiti, mummies from Egypt, and golems from Jewish lore all become angered when greedy or evil men degrade and dishonor their cultural conventions. Whether it is an archeologist who disobeys the inscription's warning on a tomb, a purposeful voodoo reincarnation at the hands of a Haitian priestess, or a well-intentioned rabbi whose creation goes terribly wrong, it is the pursuit of the secrets of life that morally bankrupts and blinds these characters to what it means to be human.

Mummies

Many of civilization's strongest religious and cultural beliefs are expressed in how the dead are prepared for burial and then laid for their final rest. The intricate ceremony and richness of the preparation and process of mummification in ancient Egypt caught the fancy of Western society centuries ago. Equally engrossed and repelled by the Egyptians' preparations for the afterlife in the Land of the Dead, the Western imagination has romanticized and embellished ancient Egyptian culture and beliefs in both literature and film.

In most mummy fiction there is a communion between the past and the present and the mysteries of life after death. It is the confrontation and exploration of our fears about the finality and permanence of death that makes mummy literature appealing. The first known mummy story in the English language was written in 1827 by Jane Webb Loundun. Entitled *Mummy! or A Tale of the Twenty-Second Century,* the novel propels us to the year 2126, when the mummified King Cheops is reanimated.[1] However, our modern notions of the mummy originated in 1923, when King Tutankhamen's tomb was opened by British archeologists Howard Carter and Lord Carnarvon. The press sensationalized the discovery by reporting a curse associated with the tomb and the doom that was imminent for those who dared enter it. Shortly after the dig was complete, Lord Carnarvon died, and public speculation about the ancient curse inspired a wave of mummy novels and films. The most significant of these was the classic 1932 film *The Mummy,* with Boris Karloff playing Imhotep, who is awakened by the reading aloud of Thoth's Scroll.

The mummy retains a flicker of humanity rare among monsters. Like the vampire, the mummy has evolved into a romantic creature who is capable of love as well as being a frightening, vengeful creature. This variation is captured in Hammer Films' 1959 version of *The Mummy* starring Christopher Lee as Kharis, a more erotic and violent mummy who is in love with his princess and is determined to bring her back to life.

Because of the public's fascination with all things Egyptian, mummies periodically reappear in film and novels, but they seem to be waning. Douglas Winter points out in his introduction to *Prime Evil* that "gone too are the survivals of past cultures—the mummies, the golems, the creatures from black lagoons; they cannot survive in a no-deposit, no-return society whose concept of ancient history is, more often than not, the 1950s."[2] As a result, the mummy has fairly consistent characteristics but is not a deeply explored subgenre within horror fiction. According to most plots, the mummy has been embalmed and buried alive, longs for his lost love, and is revived by the Scroll of Thoth being read aloud or by the life-giving juice of tana leaves. This is not to deny that there is some excellent mummy horror fiction, but lovers of ancient Egypt will find more choices in the suspense mysteries written by such authors as Elizabeth Peters, Lynda S. Robinson, Michael Pearce, and P. C. Dohery; and in historical fiction set in ancient Egypt by such authors as Pauline Gedge, Christian Jacq, Wilbur Smith, and Judith Tarr.

Zombies

Early zombie tales, generally set in the West Indies, have the creature revived by elaborate voodoo ceremonies. Lacking a will of their own, these sleepwalking automatons are made to serve the evil master who reanimated them from their graves. A common theme in this subgenre is that technology and human nature are incompatible; many zombies are revived by quasi-scientific means, including the use of powers from outer space in some of the most far-fetched science fiction stories.

Our popular notions of the zombie as a monster probably originate more from the big screen than from literature, with such classic films as *White Zombie* with Bela Lugosi and Val Lewton's *I Walk with a Zombie*. Then, in 1968, filmmaker George Romero produced *Night of the Living Dead*, a shocking, low-budget horror flick loosely based on Richard Matheson's vampire novella *I Am Legend* about flesh-eating zombies who take over the world. The zombie has provided additional fodder for contemporary novels and films due to its potential for symbolism and cautionary horrific predictions about the state of conformity of the mindless masses. "We may call them zombies, but as a character in George A. Romero's *Day of the Dead* says, 'They're us.'"[3]

Golems

The golem is a monster found in early Jewish folktales. The story of the golem serves as a cautionary tale about the limits of human power. This soulless clay creature was a natural forerunner of movie monsters such as Frankenstein's creation, and his early cinematic appearances established many of the traditions of the horror film. Interest in the golem legend among writers and artists became evident in the early twentieth century, when the golem captured the imagination of writers active in Austria, Czechoslovakia, and Germany. An outstanding work in this regard is *Der Golem* (1915) by the Bavarian writer Gustav Meyrink, who spent many years in Prague. Meyrink's book, notable for its detailed description and nightmare atmosphere, was a terrifying allegory about man's reduction to an automaton by the pressures of modern society. The most famous and effective portrayal of the golem was in the 1920 German film *Der Golem* (*The Golem*) by Paul Wegener.[4] Wegener's golem is brought to life by Rabbi Loew to protect the Jews in Prague. Loew's servant uses the golem for evil, however, and things go very wrong.

Many of these monster stories are a version of humanity's quest for the eternal, and it is the search for this hidden knowledge that brings about the destruction of man. Mummy, zombie, and golem tales tend to be cautionary stories warning that we should not step into God's domain or defy the customs and traditions of the land.

Barker, Clive. *The Damnation Game.* 1985.

> Marty Strauss, the bodyguard to wealthy and powerful Joseph Whitehead, discovers that the demon Mamoulian the Cardplayer has resurrected the dead to collect the soul of his employer, who has reneged on the bargain between the two.

Bester, Alfred. *Golem 100.* 1980.

> Trying to raise the Devil, a group of women unwittingly call up a monstrous creature, Golem 100, bent on bringing obliteration and mayhem to those who cross his path.

Boothby, Guy. *Pharos the Egyptian*. 1899.

An evil sorcerer conjures a plague that will destroy all civilization. One man knows how it is spread and can stop it only if he faces Pharos the Egyptian, an ancient mummy.

Grant, Charles. *The Long Night of the Grave*. 1986.

Once a man and brought back to life through a ceremony using ancient Egyptian artifacts from Isle Hall, a monster is unleashed to wreak havoc upon the streets of Oxrun Station.

Jones, Stephen, ed. *Mammoth Book of Zombies*. 1993.

This is a collection of short stories with contributions by Clive Barker, David J. Schow, Robert Bloch, Graham Masterston, Ramsey Campbell, and others, all featuring the reanimated undead.

King, Stephen. *Pet Sematary*. 1983.

A family relocates from Chicago to rural Maine looking for a more peaceful life, but what they actually find is that they now live near a cemetery where long-buried pets rise from the dead to terrorize them.

Little, Bentley. *The Walking*. 2000.

After his father dies and transforms into a "walker"—one of an army of zombies who are instinctively traveling to the remote deserts of Arizona—private investigator Miles Huerdeen is called into action to discover what ancient evil is reanimating the dead, drawing them across country, and what will happen when the zombies reach their destination.

Paine, Michael. *Cities of the Dead*. 1988.

Egyptologist Howard Carter comes to Cairo to study Egypt's culture and tombs, but he discovers ancient secrets and heinous rituals tied to the historical mummification and burial of the young king Tutankhamen.

Pronzini, Bill, ed. *Mummy! A Chrestomathy of Cryptology*. 1980.

An anthology of short stories by Edgar Allan Poe, Tennessee Williams, Arthur Conan Doyle, Robert Bloch, and others delves into the embalming arts and the belief in life after death.

Reaves, Michael. *Voodoo Child*. 1998.

See chapter 10, "Demonic Possession."

Rice, Anne. *The Mummy, or Ramses the Damned*. 1989.

Unearthed by an archeologist, King Ramses II reawakens in Edwardian London. Julie Stratford, the archeologist's daughter, grows to love him and helps him adjust to the modern world, but having drunk the elixir of life, he is tormented by the curse that certain hungers (for food, wine, and women) can never be satisfied.

Simmons, Dan. *Summer of Night*. 1991.

A monstrous evil is stalking the children of the small town of Elm Haven, Illinois. A group of young boys decides to investigate the disappearance of one of their schoolmates only to discover they must destroy the sinister creature before they become its next victims.

Somtow, S. P. *Darker Angels*. 1998.

A mysterious one-eyed voodoo priest ventures to raise dead soldiers from the battlefields of the Civil War in a sweeping novel that features a cast of characters ranging from Edgar Allan Poe, Abraham Lincoln, and Lord Byron to the New Orleans voodoo queen, Marie Laveau.

Stoker, Bram. *The Jewel of the Seven Stars*. 1906.

After an Egyptologist mistakenly disturbs an ancient mummy, his beautiful daughter becomes possessed by the awakened soul of the mummy. Bringing the mummy back to life is the only way to save her.

Stone, Del, Jr. *Dead Heat*. 1996.

After a botched genetic research experiment infects the world and raises the dead as zombies with a taste for human flesh, one zombie, Hitch, who has his mental capabilities still intact, motorcycles across country to find the evil zombie leader known as the Golem.

Wiesel, Elie. *The Golem*. 1983.

As seen through the eyes of a gravedigger who claims to have witnessed the golem's miracles, a creature of clay is given life by the mysterious sixteenth-century Rabbi Yehuda Loew of Prague. The golem is not a soulless monster but a figure of intuition, intelligence, and compassion who may yet return to protect the Jews from their enemies.

NOTES

The epigraph for this chapter is from Seth Holt, director of the film *Blood from the Mummy's Tomb*. He is quoted in Tom Hutchinson and Roy Pickard, *Horror: A History of Horror Movies* (Secaucus, N.J.: Chartwell, 1984), 68.

1. Paula Guran, "Return of the Mummy: Part I," http://www.darkecho/ horroronline/mummy1.html.
2. Douglas E. Winter, ed., *Prime Evil: New Stories by the Masters of Modern Horror* (New York: New American Library, 1988), 5.
3. Winter, *Prime Evil,* 5.
4. Hutchinson and Pickard, *Horror,* 108–9.

6

Vampires

Dracula Will Never Die

To die . . . to be really dead . . . that must be glorious.
—Bram Stoker, *Dracula*

Death and sexual ambivalence have long been the cornerstones of the deepest fears that lurk in the darkest shadows of our psyche. The horror genre and, uniquely, the morally depraved vampire are conducive to an eminent confrontation and exploration of these fears. Alternately haunting and tantalizing, this predator who subsists on human blood draws us to examine our own humanity. The vampire Dr. Weyland in *The Vampire Tapestry* explains: "Many creatures are dying in ways too dreadful to imagine. I am part of the world; I listen to the pain. You people claim to be above all that. You deafen yourselves with your own noise and pretend there's nothing to hear. Then these screams enter your dreams, and you have to seek therapy because you have lost the nerve to listen."

Atmosphere, being the most important literary element in all horror fiction, is uniquely expressed in this subgenre. The horrific vampire story is dependent on the author's ability to create a believable and tantalizing *feel*. It is the appropriately placed crescendo and plateau that create the sought-after spine-tingling sensation. In most vampire literature, there is a communion of the vampire motif and eroticism in the creation of this ambiance. The sexual attraction of the vampire legend hinted at in early literature is now quite overt. The vampire's ardent, insatiable need to feed adds to the mystic macabre. The sensuous action of taking blood from another beautifully lends an erotic element to Anne Rice's books as she pulls us into the vampires' mysterious world. The vampire legend has probably provided more fodder for contemporary horror novels and films than has any other theme due to its psychological suggestiveness and erotic potential, and writers and producers have been quick to explore its possibilities.

The vampire of today's fiction bears little resemblance to the frightful bloodsucking creatures found in history and folklore. In early purported vampirism, it was a common belief that individuals who were of shady character (murderers or criminals) or had violent deaths were more susceptible to return from the dead to feed on the living. Unlike the romanticized, emotionally tormented monster that has emerged since the suave portrayals of Bram Stoker's *Dracula,* the original accounts of vampires were of hideous, partially decayed creatures who attacked living relatives and neighbors rather than beautiful aristocratic damsels in distress. F. W. Murnau's 1922 silent film *Nosferatu* portrays Dracula more like an animal than a human being. He has pointy ears, menacing fingernails, and grotesque fangs that are so creepy the viewer is torn between repulsion and morbid fascination.

When Bram Stoker died in 1912, he left behind one of the two great figures in horror fiction, Count Dracula (the other being Mary Shelley's Frankenstein). First published in 1897, *Dracula* became enormously popular; the book has never been out of print and has been translated into every major language in the world.[1] Since the character entered the public domain, there have been endless variations and embellishments on this vampire in both literature and film. Count Dracula's influence on motion pictures is simply incalculable, and he has also inspired countless works of literature.[2]

Over time the vampire has evolved into a romantic creature, until most of us now envision a Hungarian-accented Bela Lugosi or Anne Rice's self-loathing Louis when we think of the undead. However, the vampire is as varied as the prolific imaginations that created him. With different personifications and characteristics, the vampire has no one dominant persona. He—or she—may have fangs, but not always; light may be fatal, but some vampires live normal lives during the day; some kill their mortal meal while feeding, while others just stun their victims; some pass the vampirism on to their quarry, but others simply enjoy a meal, rendering their prey momentarily bewildered; some are disgusted with their need to drink blood and struggle against their cursed immortality, while others see themselves as a more advanced species, higher on the food chain than mere humans. The one constant that stays true to all vampire lore, film, and literature is the blood connection; the need to drink mortal blood (animal or human) to maintain the vampire's long or eternal life.

Through chilling legends, movies, and novels, vampires have remained close to our hearts, or only a hair-raising breath away from the back of our necks. Readers' advisors need to be aware that the vampire has crossed all genres and will appeal to a wide audience. Responding to this fact, paranormal romance authors such as Amanda Ashley, Linda Lael Miller, and Christine Feehan have branched out from the horror genre to emphasize the sensuality of their flawed vampire heroes, and P. N. Elrod and Tanya Huff have created imaginative detective/mystery series featuring vampires.

(Note: Due to Anne Rice's popularity, for quick reference, we have included all of her epic vampire tales here in series order. The appendix, "The Big Three," provides a brief biographical sketch of Rice and a complete list of works by her.)

Baker, Nancy. *Kiss of the Vampire/The Night Insider.* 1993.

> In a sensual and swift-moving thriller, Ardeth Alexander, a graduate student from Toronto, is abducted and imprisoned. To her horror Ardeth realizes the purpose of her abduction is to sustain, with her blood, her fellow prisoner, who turns out to be a fifteenth-century Russian aristocrat and vampire.

Bergstrom, Elaine. *Blood Alone.* 1990.

> In pre-World War II Europe, Paul Stoddard falls in love with a beautiful Austrian woman who is also a member of a family of vampires. Together they become involved in World War II and fight the menace of Nazism. (Prequel to *Shattered Glass,* 1989.)

Bloch, Robert. *Midnight Pleasures.* 1987.

> This mixture of fourteen suspense, fantasy, and horror short stories explores a cross-section of the horror subgenres.

Brite, Poppy Z. *Lost Souls*. 1992.

A troubled teenage boy named Nothing, who is born of a vampire, searches for his true family in this graphic coming-of-age story. After running away he meets other vampires in a blood- and sex-filled spree of adventures. Not for the weak of stomach.

Brite, Poppy Z., ed. *Love in Vein: Twenty Original Tales of Vampiric Erotica*. 1994. / *Love in Vein II*. 1998.

These are collections of erotic and graphic original stories written by a range of authors celebrating the sensual fantasies of the vampiric myth.

Charnas, Suzy McKee. *The Vampire Tapestry*. 1980.

This novella, set partly in New Mexico, introduces the modern-day vampire Dr. Edward Weyland, an anthropology professor who attempts to remain true to his species by staying emotionally detached from his human prey, whom he prefers to consider as "livestock."

Collins, Nancy. *Sunglasses after Dark*. 1989.

In the summer of 1969, Sonja Blue gets kidnapped, transformed into a vampire, and then seeks revenge. This is a violent, erotic variation on the traditional supernatural vampire/vampire hunter tale. (Sonja Blue Trilogy, 1.) Sequels: *In the Blood*, 1992; *Paint It Black*, 1995.

Elrod, P. N., ed. *Dracula in London*. 2001.

A collaboration of authors offering sixteen stories that elaborate on the life and myths of Bram Stoker's Dracula.

Hambly, Barbara. *Those Who Hunt the Night*. 1988.

Returning home to find his wife in a strange coma, Professor James Asher is commissioned by London's oldest vampire, Simon Ysidro, to find out who has been hunting vampires by day, tearing open their coffins, and exposing them to lethal daylight.

Hamilton, Laurell K. *Obsidian Butterfly*. 2000.

This is the ninth in the comic horror Anita Blake Series. Anita travels to Albuquerque, New Mexico, to help Edward track down a vicious monster responsible for a series of grotesque murders. (Anita Blake Vampire Hunter Series, 9.) Titles in series: *Guilty Pleasures*, 1993; *The*

Laughing Corpse, 1994; *Circus of the Damned,* 1995; *The Lunatic Café,* 1996; *Bloody Bones,* 1996; *The Killing Dance,* 1997; *Burnt Offerings,* 1998; *Blue Moon,* 1998; *Obsidian Butterfly,* 2000; *Narcissus in Chains,* 2001; *Cerulean Sins,* 2003.

Huff, Tanya. *Blood Pact.* 1993.

Going progressively blind, ex-cop Vicki Nelson and her 450-year-old vampire partner and lover attempt to uncover a dark conspiracy surrounding the sudden death of Vicki's mother. When the body disappears, Vicki discovers that things are not as they seem at the hospital where her mother had worked. (Blood Series, 4.) Titles in series: *Blood Price,* 1991; *Blood Trail,* 1992; *Blood Lines,* 1993; *Blood Pact,* 1993; *Blood Debt,* 1997.

Jones, Stephen, ed.
The Mammoth Book of Dracula: Vampire Tales for the New Millennium. 1997.

Celebrating Dracula's 100th anniversary, authors such as Kim Newman, Brian Stableford, and Ramsey Campbell offer thirty-three stories that feature the master vampire, Dracula.

The Mammoth Book of Vampire Stories by Women. 2001.

This is an anthology of thirty-four erotic vampire tales by both classic and contemporary authors, including Nancy Collins, Tanya Huff, Tanith Lee, and Poppy Z. Brite.

Kalogridis, Jeanne. *Children of the Vampire.* 1995.

This highly erotic historical novel is a prequel to Bram Stoker's *Dracula.* It is the story of Arkady Tsepesh, great-grandnephew of Vlad, Count Dracula. For the last four centuries, the firstborn male has received the vampire bite, but now the family curse is drawing Arkady's son, Stefan, to Vlad's castle in Transylvania, and Arkady must intervene before he too suffers the fate of vampirism. (Diaries of the Family Dracul Series, 2.) Titles in series: *Covenant of the Vampire,* 1994; *Children of the Vampire,* 1995; *Lord of the Vampires,* 1996.

King, Stephen. *Salem's Lot.* 1975.

The streets of a small Maine town are empty by day because the citizens of Jerusalem's Lot have all become vampires. This novel is part classic horror and part social commentary on the problems within insular communities in America.

Lumley, Brian. *Deadspeak*. 1990.

Led by Harry Keogh, the "Necroscope" (one who speaks to the dead), a team of vampire hunters belonging to an ultrasecret division of the British secret service fight against a resurrected master vampire's plans to use his undead soldiers to conquer the world.

Martin, George R. R. *Fevre Dream*. 1982.

On an 1850s Mississippi steamboat, Joshua York, who combines features of the werewolf and vampire, becomes partners with Captain Abner Marsh. This is a bloody and graphic encounter of the "good vampire versus bad vampire" as the ideals and philosophy of York and his vampire adversary, Damon Julian, collide.

Matheson, Richard. *I Am Legend*. 1954.

In a treatment of vampirism as an infectious disease, these short stories tell of a mysterious plague that has swept the planet, and Robert Neville seems to be the only man left who is immune. As the sole survivor, Neville is forced to outwit the vampires that are all after him. George Romero adapted this plot for the movie *Night of the Living Dead*.

Newman, Kim. *Anno Dracula*. 1992.

In an alternative history of the 1880s, Queen Victoria has married Vlad Tepes, better known as Count Dracula. Jack the Ripper, who is none other than Stoker's character Dr. John (Jack) Seward, is killing the vampire prostitutes living in London. Genevieve Dieuxdonne, a vampire detective, is assigned to hunt down Jack. In this vivid and graphic tale there are also appearances of Mycroft Holmes, Dr. Jekyll, and other Victorian literature favorites.

RICE, ANNE. CHRONICLES OF THE VAMPIRES

Interview with the Vampire. 1976.

In an interview with a boy reporter, the eighteenth-century plantation owner Louis Pointe du Lac makes his confessions of how he came to be a vampire and his consequent torment and guilt.

The Vampire Lestat. 1985.

Lestat, having risen after fifty years, awakens in the 1980s to the wonders of the modern world. He becomes a rock star and breaks centuries of self-imposed vampire silence by penning an autobiography of his childhood in eighteenth-century France and how he came to be a vampire.

The Queen of the Damned. 1988.

Akasha, Queen of the Damned, awakens after 6,000 years of sleep. Once the queen of the Nile, Akasha is now intent on saving mankind from itself. Then there is Lestat, whose successful singing career has angered hundreds of other vampires. Throw in the twins, Maharet and Mekare, who are haunting dreams the world over and you have the ingredients for an all-out vampire showdown.

The Tale of the Body Thief. 1992.

Lonely and full of doubts, Lestat makes a deal with Raglan James, a Body Thief who can switch souls with another being, and who also happens to be a very talented con artist. Against the advice of his friends, Lestat agrees to temporarily switch bodies with the man, so that he can once again experience being mortal.

Memnoch the Devil. 1995.

Lestat searches for Dora, a mortal with whom he has become infatuated at the same time he is being stalked by a shadowy figure who turns out to be Memnoch, the Devil. Memnoch presents Lestat with unimagined opportunities: to witness creation and to visit purgatory. Lestat must ponder the ultimate question of what he believes to be good and evil.

The Vampire Armand. 1998.

Set in fifteenth-century Constantinople, Armand recounts his memories of his childhood abduction from Kiev, how he was sold to a Venetian artist and vampire, Marius, how he was transformed into a vampire, and the subsequent love affair he had with his mentor.

Merrick. 2000.

The vampires Lestat and Louis and the dead vampire child Claudia are introduced to the Mayfair Witches. Louis, obsessed with raising

Claudia's ghost to make amends, elicits Merrick Mayfair's help to conjure up her spirit for one last visit.

Blood and Gold. 2001.

Marius, the mentor of Lestat, the creator of Armand, and the lover of Pandora, tells of his 2,000-year existence and how he became the burdened protector of Akasha and Enkil, the very first parents of the vampires.

RICE, ANNE. NEW TALES OF THE VAMPIRES

Pandora. 1998.

The vampire David Talbot approaches beautiful Pandora and convinces her to write down the story of her remarkable 2,000-year life, from her mortal years as the only daughter of a wealthy Roman senator circa 15 B.C. to her exile in Antioch, her initiation into the worship of the great goddess Isis, and her turbulent love affair with the Venetian vampire Marius.

Vittorio, the Vampire. 1999.

Vittorio, a vampire from the Italian Golden Age, is seduced by the vampire Ursula, the most beautiful of his supernatural enemies. With vengeance in mind, he enters the Court of the Ruby Grail and finds himself increasingly disquieted by his attraction to the mysterious Ursula.

Saberhagen, Fred. *The Dracula Tape.* 1975.

Intent upon vindicating himself, Count Dracula retells the events of Bram Stoker's novel from his point of view, portraying Van Helsing as the villain. (Dracula Series, 1.) Titles in series: *The Dracula Tape*, 1975; *Old Friend of the Family,* 1979; *Thorn,* 1980; *Dominion,* 1982; *The Holmes-Dracula File,* 1989; *Matter of Taste,* 1990; *A Question of Time,* 1992; *Séance for a Vampire,* 1994; *A Sharpness on the Neck,* 1996.

Simmons, Dan. *Carrion Comfort.* 1989.

Told through several points of view, long-term rivals Nina, Melanie, and Willi have the psychic ability to drive others to violence by sheer mental force and can extend their lives indefinitely by feeding on the deaths they cause.

Somtow, S. P. *Vampire Junction.* 1984.

Frozen at age thirteen for almost 2,000 years, the teen rock star and innocent-looking vampire Timmy Valentine struggles to come to terms with the feelings of guilt and empathy he feels for his mortal victims. (Timmy Valentine Series, 1.) Sequels: *Valentine,* 1992; *Vanitas,* 1995.

Stoker, Bram. *Dracula.* 1897.

See chapter 3, "The Classics."

Strieber, Whitley. *The Hunger.* 1981.

Miriam Blaylock is of an ancient race of vampires that possess telepathic talents. In her isolation she craves human company, but her attempts to create an immortal companion end with tragic results.

Sturgeon, Theodore. *Some of Your Blood.* 1961.

In a psychological study of blood fetishism, the Army psychiatrist Philip Outerbridge conducts George Smith's therapy. Much of the story is told through medical transcripts and documents that reveal George's vampirism.

Yarbro, Chelsea Quinn.
Hotel Transylvania. 1978.

In mid-eighteenth-century Paris, the Comte de Saint-Germain, a suave vampire who is also the newest member of Louis XV's court, helps his great love, Madelaine de Montalia, escape from a cult of devil worshipers. (Saint-Germain Series, 1.) Titles in series: *Hotel Transylvania,* 1978; *The Palace,* 1978; *Blood Games,* 1979; *Path of the Eclipse,* 1981; *Tempting Fate,* 1982; *The Saint-Germain Chronicles,* 1983; *Out of the House of Life,* 1990; *Darker Jewels,* 1993; *Better in the Dark,* 1993; *Mansions of Darkness,* 1996; *Writ in Blood,* 1997; *Blood Roses,* 1998; *Communion Blood,* 1999; *Come Twilight,* 2000; *A Feast in Exile,* 2001; *Night Blooming,* 2002.

The Soul of an Angel. 1999.

Seduced by Dracula's sensual powers, Fenice Zucchar, the daughter of a wealthy shipowner, seeks freedom from a life of boredom. She is lured to Dracula's mountain domain, where she is introduced to Kelene, one of the Dark Lord's other vampire brides. (Sisters of the Night Series, 2.) Prequel: *The Angry Angel*, 1998.

NOTES

1. Stoker's Dracula Organisation, Dublin, http://www.bramstokercentre.org/dracula.htm.
2. Stoker's Dracula Organisation.

7

Werewolves and Animals of Terror
The Beast Walks among Us

The fish moved close, still cruising back and forth but closing the gap between itself and the boat by a few feet with every passage. Then it stopped, twenty or twenty-five feet away, and for a second seemed to lie motionless in the water, aimed directly at the boat. The tail dropped beneath the surface; the dorsal fin slid backward and vanished; and the great head reared up, mouth open in a slack, savage grin, eyes black and abysmal. —Peter Benchley, *Jaws*

Throughout history, man has revered and even worshiped animals. The more powerful and predacious the beast, the more respect it tended to elicit. Faced with powerful predators, people incorporated them into their lore. Powerful or dangerous people were thought to assume the characteristics of animals, and it was believed that beasts could take on even greater strength and menace than were natural to their species and become a threat to humanity. Threatening animals, a popular theme in horror literature, address our primal fears of being attacked by a wild beast, or conversely, of being attacked by an animal that is usually controlled by man. The idea that Fido could become a ferocious killer or that a naturally shy fish could evolve into an aggressive hunter terrorizing summer swimmers is both disturbing and the stuff of which horror is made.

One of the most fearsome and well-known animals in folklore is the wolf, and certain legends center on the transformation of a man into a werewolf (lycanthropy). Shape-shifting is deeply rooted in folklore and myth throughout the world. The legendary twins Romulus and Remus who founded Rome are said to have been nursed by a she-wolf and acquired her ferocity as a result. The folklore of Europe, India, China, and the North American Indians is rich in tales of transformation. In the classic legend of the werewolf, a man who has been bitten by a wolf is periodically transformed (under a full moon) into a fur-covered, snarling beast who abandons his humanity for the bestial appearance and behavior of the animal.

Perhaps this animal caught the imagination because, throughout much of human history, wolf packs were a real menace to rural farmers and their livestock. As in vampire literature, over time this fearful predator has evolved into a romantic creature with a correlation made between the werewolf motif and eroticism. The same sensuous action of the vampire's bite lends an erotic undertone to the passing of werewolfery to this creature's victims. Lon Chaney Jr.'s portrayal of Lawrence Talbot in *The Wolf Man* (1941) illustrates the romanticized, emotionally tortured monster and prisoner of the full moon that reluctantly emerges.

Wolves are not the only animals that have inspired horror fiction. There is a massive amount of animal horror available. Writers have created attacking sharks, dogs, cats, birds, spiders—the list is endless. We have offered but a sampling here. It is important to note, however, that there is much more transformative literature involving animals in works of fantasy and within the regular fiction collection.

Werewolves

Armstrong, Kelly.
> *Bitten*. 2001.
>
> Elena Michaels is the only female werewolf in existence. After ten years of living with the pack, Elena moves to Toronto, seeking a normal life among humans. When some mutts (werewolves not living in a pack) start torturing and murdering, Elena is called upon to help track them down and end their killing spree before the werewolf clan is exposed.
>
> *Stolen*. 2003.
>
> Tycoon Ty Winslow is collecting all the supernatural species that secretly live among humans, including vampires, witches, demons, and

werewolves. Elena Michaels, the only female werewolf in the world, is kidnapped by Winslow and needs all her cunning and wit to outsmart him until the pack can find and rescue her. (Sequel to *Bitten*.)

Borchardt, Alice.
The Silver Wolf. 1998.

In this book Alice Borchardt, who is Anne Rice's older sister, introduces Regeane, a distant relation to Charlemagne and secret shape-shifter living in Rome during the Dark Ages. Caught in the politics of the time, Regeane struggles to reconcile her human and wolf natures. (Wolf Series, 1.)

Night of the Wolf. 1999.

As Julius Caesar sets his sights on conquering Britain, werewolf pack leader Maeniel is captured and trained as a gladiator. He teams up with the warrior Dryas as the fateful ides of March approach. (Wolf Series, 2.)

Wolf King. 2000.

The eighth-century werewolves Maeniel and Regeane find themselves caught in the middle of a war between King Desiderus and Charlemagne. The war of men threatens to destroy the werewolves' way of life, and when Maeniel is captured it is up to Regeane to set things right. (Wolf Series, 3.)

Boyd, Donna.
The Passion. 1998.

After the murders of three werewolves in Manhattan, 120-year-old pack leader Alexander Devoncroix reveals to his son a tightly guarded family secret involving his relationship with human Tessa LeGuerre. Tessa, allowed into the werewolf community, learns of the power the superior werewolves hold over human society. Tragedy falls on the pack and Tessa when she becomes entangled in the evil plots of Alexander's brother to rid the world of the human race. (Werewolf Series, 1.)

The Promise. 1999.

Alaskan wildlife photographer Hannah Braselton North discovers a wounded wolf at a helicopter crash site, as well as a diary containing the memoirs of Matise Devoncroix telling of a powerful hidden race of werewolves. As Hannah delves deeper into the memoirs, she becomes convinced that her patient is one of them—no common wolf, but a relation of Devoncroix. (Werewolf Series, 2.)

Cacek, P. D. *Canyons.* 2000.

After being rescued from a holdup by what she believes is a werewolf, tabloid writer Cat Moselle writes an article for her paper that puts Lucas and his entire Denver shape-shifting clan in danger of exposure. To make matters worse, another werewolf pack is killing in their territory, and Lucas is forced to team with Cat in order to keep his clan's existence unknown and therefore safe.

DiSilvestro, Roger L. *Ursula's Gift.* 1988.

Stanley Merriwether is a plump good-natured man with little self-confidence. After he intervenes in a dispute involving a prostitute being beaten by her pimp, the woman repays his aid by biting him on the back, making him a werewolf. Stanley likes the change: he is losing weight, women are attracted to him for the first time, and he is developing a backbone when dealing with his overbearing, big game-hunting father. However, a full moon is coming and his father has declared that Stanley is to be his next trophy.

Holland, David. *Murcheston: The Wolf's Tale.* 2000.

The Victorian Londoner Edgar Lenoir, Duke of Darnley, has a passion for hunting. After surviving a nasty run-in with a wolf, he find himself metamorphosing into a wolf, losing his humanity while being consumed with the animal desires of the beast he is to become.

Jones, Stephen, ed. *The Mammoth Book of Werewolves.* 1994.

Part of a larger group of anthologies on various horror subgenres, this collection focuses on the essential werewolf stories. Works by authors like Clive Barker, Ramsey Campbell, Graham Masterton, and Kim Newman are included in this accessible and satisfying work.

King, Stephen. *Cycle of the Werewolf.* 1983.

A Maine werewolf's escapes are recounted in twelve tales, one for each month's full moon. This is a classic werewolf tale, combining well-known legend and King's superior storytelling style. Editions with intricate illustrations by Berni Wrightson enhance the story.

Klause, Annette Curtis. *Blood and Chocolate.* 1997.

Living in a Maryland suburb, sixteen-year-old Vivian Gandillon falls in love with sensitive and gentle Aiden. But Vivian is a werewolf and Aiden is human, making this coming-of-age story a bit complicated.

Murphy, Pat. *Nadya: The Wolf Chronicles.* 1997.

In the 1830s Missouri wilderness, Nadya discovers she is a shape-changer or werewolf. After her parents are tragically killed, Nadya's saga begins as she heads west, teaming up with Elizabeth Metcalf and orphaned Jenny while seeking acceptance for who and what she really is.

Saul, John. *Guardian.* 1993.

In the midst of marital troubles, Mary Anne Carpenter's best friend dies in a mysterious accident, leaving Mary Anne guardian of her thirteen-year-old son, Joey. Taking her two children to a vast ranch in Idaho to care for Joey, Mary Anne thinks she might have found a perfect new home until tragedy strikes when campers in the nearby campgrounds are found brutally murdered. To make matters worse, Joey disappears at night for hours and is acting very strange.

Smith, Thomas. *Thor.* 1992.

Thor, a German shepherd, tells the story of his pack, the family of five that he lives with and is bound to protect. They are threatened with the arrival of Uncle Ted, who unbeknownst to the family is a werewolf. Fortunately, Thor knows, and as the moon gets fuller and Uncle Ted creepier, Thor becomes more intent on protecting his pack no matter what the cost.

Somtow, S. P. *Moon Dance.* 1989.

Flashing between the 1960s and the late 1880s, schizophrenic werewolf Johnny Kincaid tells of his youth in the Dakota Territory, where the Old World has a bloody meeting with the New. He recalls the great battles that took place when the nearly extinct European werewolf von Wolfen family first immigrated to the plains of the West and encountered a small Lakota tribal group, the revered People of the Wolf.

Stableford, Brian.

The Werewolves of London. 1990.

Bitten by a snake during a visit to a remote area in Egypt, young David Lydyard finds himself plagued with strange and extravagant visions. Gabriel Gill also possesses similar visionary powers. The two find themselves caught in a secret war between the forces of werewolves, occultists, and fallen angels. (Werewolves of London Trilogy, 1.)

The Angel of Pain. 1991.

In 1893 London, David Lydyard is still suffering from a twenty-year-old bite he received from an asp-like snake in Egypt that infused him with the soul of the Sphinx. Used by the Sphinx to battle her rival angels (who also use human pawns) to gain world domination, Lydyard is forced to join the werewolves of London to battle the greater evil, all the while waging an inner battle with the Angel of Pain that can release him from his physical pain and visions. (Werewolves of London Trilogy, 2.)

The Carnival of Destruction. 1994.

At the climax of World War I, David Lydyard is again involved with the werewolves of London, as the fallen angels seek to determine their future by pitting their energies against each other using the men on the battlefields like pawns in a game of chess. (Werewolves of London Trilogy, 3.)

Strieber, Whitley. *The Wolfen.* 1978.

The wolfen have made a huge mistake by savagely killing two New York City policemen. Now they are being hunted by Detective George Wilson and his partner, Detective Becky Neff. The survival of the fittest will be determined as the battle lines are drawn between the animals and the humans.

Tessier, Thomas. *The Night Walker.* 1979.

A young American, Bobby Ives is living in London when he finds himself in direct and agonizing conflict with an unknown power that seeks to transform him into a werewolf capable of horrifying violence.

Animals of Terror

Alten, Steve.

Meg. 1997.

Jonas Taylor was the only survivor of what he believes was a real Meg—the prehistoric *Carcharodon megalodon,* a massive ancestor of the great white shark. Now something has stirred Meg from her abyss and she is migrating to the surface. Only Taylor seems to recognize how powerful and ferocious this ancient creature can be.

The Trench. 1999.

The Mariana Trench in the Pacific Ocean is the home of a twenty-ton megalodon, a prehistoric killing shark that has a taste for human blood. Paleobiologist Jonas Taylor must once again face the creature down in the Trench in order to stop its terror along the California coast.

Bakis, Kirsten. *Lives of the Monster Dogs.* 1997.

In 1897 the German scientist Augustus Rank engineered an advanced race of soldier dogs. By 2008 they have evolved into hyper-intelligent canines that walk on their hind legs and, fitted with voice-boxes, can communicate with people. Forced to leave their home, they move to New York City and meet Cleo Pira, who digs into Rank's past to discover that his race of "monster dogs" is doomed for destruction.

Benchley, Peter. *Jaws.* 1974.

In the hit novel that made us think twice before putting so much as a toe in the water, Benchley tells of a great white shark that leaves a bloody trail along a coastal resort town. Police chief Marty Brody is forced to hunt the giant shark down before he kills again.

Crichton, Michael.

Jurassic Park. 1993.

InGen, a genetic engineering firm, has succeeded in cloning fifteen species of dinosaurs. Jurassic Park is an amusement park off the coast of Costa Rica that features real live dinosaurs. When the dinosaurs escape their barricaded area, the scientists and special guests must run for their lives.

The Lost World. 1995.

Six years after the disaster at Jurassic Park, carcasses of supposedly extinct saurians are washing ashore on a nearby island. Every critter was thought to have been destroyed, but something is out there and a group of researchers are drawn to the deserted island off the coast of Costa Rica to investigate.

du Maurier, Daphne. "The Birds." 1952.

The short story classic of the macabre on which Alfred Hitchcock based his famous film evolves around the nightmarish idea of birds turning against mankind. After a harsh winter, a farmer and his family in a rural area of England are attacked by an increasing number of hostile birds.

Elze, Winifred. *Here Kitty, Kitty.* 1997.

Woolly mammoths, saber-toothed tigers, and other extinct animals mysteriously appear in an Adirondack town. Emma Vernon and her cat, Billie, investigate how these dangerous Pleistocene-era animals are migrating from their time to ours.

Eulo, Ken, Joe Mauck, and Jeffrey Mauck. *Claw.* 1995.

Rajah, a 700-pound Siberian tiger, becomes uncharacteristically vicious and begins killing, escapes the zoo, and excites terror across the city of Los Angeles. Animal care specialist Meg Brewster discovers that a secret scientific experiment has turned Rajah into a ferocious killer and she must find him before it's too late.

Gregory, Stephen. *The Cormorant.* 1996.

After inheriting a cottage in Wales from an eccentric uncle, a young couple and their son, Harry, discover the stipulation of caring for Archie, Uncle Ian's pet cormorant. The bird embodies some vile force that drags the family into a terrifying nightmare of evil and malice.

King, Stephen. *Cujo.* 1981.

After being bitten by a rabid bat, Cujo, a 200-pound Saint Bernard, begins terrorizing his owners and a neighboring family. This terrifying tale of a pet gone mad is heightened by the well-told narrative of the lives of its victims.

Koontz, Dean. *Watchers*. 1987.

See chapter 11, "Scientific and Biomedical Horror."

Rovin, Jeff. *Vespers*. 1998.

A series of vicious bat attacks have been terrorizing New York City. Scientist Nancy Joyce and Detective Robert Gentry investigate and are caught in a life-and-death struggle with these deadly predators.

Strieber, Whitley. *The Forbidden Zone*. 1993.

In this stated homage to Lovecraft, insectlike monsters swarm over a mountain town. Brian and Loi Kelly are the first to notice something is wrong. Brian is a physicist trying to forget his past, which includes a dead wife and child. Loi is his new pregnant wife. With the help of a local reporter, will they be able to save their town from these awful insects who mesmerize and then devour their prey? Strieber includes plenty of gore here.

8

Maniacs and Other Monsters

The Killer Lurking in the Corner

Monsters have been a part of the human storytelling tradition from its inception. The proof can be seen in the large number of monstrous creatures one finds in the mythologies and religions of just about every culture. These monsters were created to help our ancestors explain the unexplainable. By injecting an amoral, supernatural being into their stories, humans were able to explain horrible occurrences such as plagues, wars, storms, fires, and earthquakes. Today, while we are still fascinated by stories of supernatural monsters, we are also increasingly drawn to tales, both fictional and true, of human monsters. All of the novels in this subgenre focus on a homicidal maniac, be it a human serial killer, an ancient spirit in the guise of man, or a supernatural being in some grotesque form. While the shape and motivation of these maniacs may vary, they are grouped together here because, for our purposes as readers' advisors, the characteristics and appeal factors of these novels are eerily similar.

The first and most basic characteristic of these works is the appearance of a tangible threat in the form of some type of maniacal killer. This may sound obvious, but it is important to note that in many horror novels the characters are physically threatened by their guilt, past deeds, or imagined terrors. These works revolve more around the characters' inner demons than around the physical threat of a killer, and are considered to be psychological horror. However, in the subgenre under discussion here, it is the maniac himself who initiates the plot's conflict, drives its action, and whose destruction the resolution is dependent upon. He can be a serial killer, as in Dean Koontz's *Intensity,* or an immortal monster in the guise of a family man, as in *Sacrifice* by John Farris. In every work of this subgenre, the maniac must be stopped, and the action will continue until the characters manage this dangerous task.

The violence inherent in these works leads us to the next characteristic of the maniac story. These are bloody books, and many are quite graphic in their descriptions. Moreover, the violence quite often leads to the death of a major character. For example, in the hunt to rid the museum of a killer monster, the characters in Douglas Preston and Lincoln Child's *The Relic* are put in grave danger and one of the hunters falls victim to the creature. The result is even more shocking in Ramsey Campbell's *One Safe Place,* when a major character does not make it through the novel's conflict alive. The monsters and maniacs portrayed in these books must be feared by the reader in order to provoke true terror. Thus, the monster spares no one in his path, sweeping the reader along for a dangerous ride.

The final characteristic of this subgenre is the complexity of the killer's motivation. While it cannot be argued that he is not committing evil acts, even the most unsympathetic serial killer has reasons for his actions. The reader is given a chance to see behind the maniac and get a glimpse into his past and the reasons for his horrifying behavior. In some cases the killer is even trying to right things himself and make up for past misdeeds, as is the case with Azriel in Anne Rice's *Servant of the Bones.* The reader may also see a monster forced to choose between continuing with his evil ways or turning to a life of good, as with David in *My Soul to Keep* by Tanarive Due. A variety of situations is represented here, but the overall message is the same; the killers populating the pages of this subgenre are not simply manifestations of pure evil; they each have a complex story of how they became so monstrous.

Maniac stories have distinct appeal factors which can either draw in or repel readers, depending on their personal preferences. Readers who enjoy stories with graphic descriptions of sex and violence will be right at home with the novels on this list. This subgenre will also appeal to readers who like complex and unpredictable plots, where flashbacks are employed frequently, likable characters are killed off, and points of view can shift without notice. Maniac novels also tend to have open endings which quite often lead to sequels. However, these same factors can also make the novels unpalatable to readers who like tamer works of horror, with simpler plot construction and closed endings.

But the biggest appeal factor here comes out of our obsession with murder. If you doubt the wide interest in serial and other killers, take a quick look at the number and circulation records of the books in your library's true crime section. Joyce Carol Oates's *Zombie* provides a perfect example of this obsession. The award-winning novel recounts the exploits of a serial killer through his diary entries; the reader is allowed to literally step inside the mind of a monster. Some readers may find it too frightening to explore these dark corners of the human mind in such realistic tales. Instead, they may prefer turning to the supernatural monsters in this subgenre. These works allow the reader to look evil in the eye with a little more distance.

Bloch, Robert. *Psycho.* 1959.

> The plot of this book, upon which the classic Hitchcock film is faithfully based, will be familiar to most readers. An exhausted Mary Crane checks into the Bates Motel. But it quickly becomes apparent that this is not your ordinary motel, and Norman Bates is not your normal motel manager. We also recommend Bloch's other maniac masterpiece, *American Gothic* (1974).

Campbell, Ramsey. *One Safe Place.* 1996.

> Suzanne Travis gets a job at an English university teaching a course on violence in film and relocates her husband, Don, a bookseller, and their twelve-year-old son, Marshall, from Florida to Manchester. However, the Travises are soon caught up in a deadly feud with the maniacal Fancy family. A widening circle of brutality soon surrounds the family and threatens their safety. *The Count of Eleven* (1992) is also a part of this subgenre.

Dobyns, Stephen. *The Church of Dead Girls.* 1997.

> In a slightly different take on traditional serial killer fare, Dobyns concentrates his attention on how a small town reacts to a series of murders within their tight-knit community. Suspicion and fear overcome this small upstate New York town as the residents try to identify the monster living among them.

Due, Tanarive. *My Soul to Keep.* 1997.

A 500-year-old African immortal man is living in modern times as David, a jazz scholar in a middle-class family. He has had many lives and loves throughout his long life, but his current situation as husband to Jessica and father to young Kira is extremely satisfying. However, David's original family of immortals asks him to sever all ties with Jessica and Kira in order to save their kind.

Epperson, S. K. *The Neighborhood.* 1995.

In this grisly novel, Epperson takes the reader into a neighborhood of evildoers including serial killers, wife beaters, and kidnappers, just to name a few. Our guide through this grotesque world of monsters and maniacs is a kindly nurse, Abra Aherns, who uncovers the grotesque and horrifying secrets about her neighbors as she works to find a kidnapped girl.

Farris, John. *Sacrifice.* 1994.

In this unique and well-written novel, perfect family man Greg Walker's strange behavior begins to worry the young daughter who idolizes him. Little does she know that he is an immortal member of a Mayan cult who, in order to keep up his immortality, must sacrifice a virgin daughter every nineteen years. As Walker prepares his unsuspecting daughter for a trip to Guatemala, local detective Will Butterbaugh tries to save the girl from her bloody fate.

Gaiman, Neil. *Neverwhere.* 1997.

Richard Mayhew is your average young Londoner, until he stops to help a young homeless girl he finds on the street. His one moment of selflessness leads Richard into "London Below," a dark and magical parallel city under the familiar streets of his hometown. But before he can return to the world above, Richard must battle monsters and henchmen, visit with a fallen angel, and find his own inner strength. *Neverwhere* is a dark fantasy masterpiece.

Harris, Thomas. *Silence of the Lambs.* 1989.

The award-winning movie starring Jodie Foster and Anthony Hopkins was made from this chilling tale. Clarice Starling is sent to the jail cell of the evil Hannibal Lecter to get his help in catching a serial killer.

Harris's superb writing takes the reader deep into the mind of a maniac. His book won a Bram Stoker Award. *Red Dragon* (1981) and *Hannibal* (1999) bookend this thriller to complete the trilogy.

King, Stephen. *Carrie*. 1974.

In King's first novel, Carrie White does not fit in anywhere—either at home or at school, but when she discovers her own telekinetic powers, she begins to use them to extract revenge. Other King titles in this subgenre include *Misery* (1988), winner of a Bram Stoker Award, and *Rose Madder* (1995).

Koontz, Dean.
Phantoms. 1983.

Dr. Jennifer Paige returns home to Snowfield, California, with her newly orphaned little sister only to find that everyone in the resort town has died of mysterious causes or disappeared completely. Jennifer and a group of diverse survivors band together to fight who, or what, is responsible. Another work by Koontz in the "monsters" category is *Midnight* (1989).

Intensity. 1995.

When Chyna Shepard, a psychology student, spends the weekend at her friend's Victorian farm house, her life is changed forever. On her first night there, Chyna witnesses the murder of everyone in the house. The rest of the novel has Chyna tracking down the killer in an attempt to save his future victims. Other titles by Koontz in the "maniacs" category include *Lightning* (1988) and *Face of Fear* (1985).

Lansdale, Joe. *The Nightrunner*. 1987.

After Becky was raped, her husband Monty takes them into the country to recover. However, the rapist's friends are out for revenge in a 1966 Cadillac and are bearing down on the couple. Throw in the God of the Razor and you have a study in pure evil.

Little, Bentley. *The Store*. 1998.

The small town of Juniper, Arizona, gets its first large chain store, named simply The Store. The citizens are excited about its arrival, but as soon as construction begins, strange things begin to happen. While life goes on as normal outside The Store, inside its walls evil lurks.

March, William. *The Bad Seed.* 1954.

See chapter 3, "The Classics."

Massie, Elizabeth. *Sineater.* 1993.

In a backwoods Virginia town, a religious sect chooses a man to absorb the sins of the dead. As a result of all the evil he is forced to burden, the sineater is not to be looked upon. However, the current sineater, Avery Barker, has broken with tradition by having a family, and someone is not very happy about that. *Sineater* won a Bram Stoker Award for best first novel.

McCabe, Patrick. *The Butcher Boy.* 1994.

Francie Brady has a tough life. He is a Catholic teenager living in near poverty in Northern Ireland. His dad drinks too much and his mom is suicidal. McCabe chronicles Brady's life as he is engulfed by hatred. The reader then stands by helplessly and watches Brady turn into a ruthless serial killer. This book is both lyrical and gruesome. *The Butcher Boy* was short-listed for England's prestigious Booker Prize.

McCammon, Robert. *Mine.* 1990.

Mary Terror, a former member of a 1960s radical group, is still living in the past twenty years later. In a drug-induced state, Mary kidnaps a baby, but its mother chases after Mary. What ensues is a horrific trip through the underworld of radical groups and the destruction left in their wake. This tale of horror and suspense climaxes with a fight between the two women over the child. *Mine* and McCammon's *Swan Song* (1996), also in this subgenre, both won Bram Stoker Awards.

Oates, Joyce Carol. *Zombie.* 1995.

Zombie tells the story of convicted sex offender turned serial killer Quentin P. in diary form. Oates convincingly puts the reader into the mind of a maniac as he strives to create the perfect "zombie," a young man he can lobotomize to be his slave. Since this work is in diary form, drawings and changes in font are employed throughout. A chilling study of the darkest corners of the human mind, *Zombie* won a Bram Stoker Award.

Pike, Christopher. *The Cold One.* 1995.

Pike is best known for his chilling books for a young adult audience, but *The Cold One* is definitely written for adults. The eponymous monster of this novel is introduced and described in the prologue. The story then follows the exploits of a varied cast of characters whose lives have been touched by this monster, ranging from a reporter to a 5,000-year-old Hindu and just about everyone in between. The many subplots and characters all intersect for a final confrontation on a beach in California. This tale is more violent and gruesome than Pike's books for young adults.

Preston, Douglas, and Lincoln Child. *The Relic.* 1995.

Days before the opening of a new exhibit on "Superstitions" at the New York Museum of Natural History, someone, or something, is committing brutal murders inside the museum. The murders appear to be the work of an Amazonian god whose history and relics are scheduled to become part of the exhibit. Can a band of museum workers stop this monster before it kills again? *The Relic* is extremely popular, was made into a successful motion picture, and has a decent sequel, *The Reliquary* (1997).

Rice, Anne. *Servant of the Bones.* 1996.

In ancient Babylon around 600 B.C., Azriel, a devoted follower of the Hebrew prophets Isaiah and Jeremiah, is sacrificed to become Servant of the Bones so that his people may return to Jerusalem. Condemned to an immortal life as a spirit forced to do the evil bidding of his master, Azriel's sacrifice for the good of his people has turned him into a monster against his will. He recounts his tale to Jonathan in an attempt to redeem himself and put an end to his master's evil reign.

Saul, John. *Black Lightning.* 1993.

At the execution of notorious serial killer Richard Kraven, the husband of journalist Anne Jeffords suffers a near-fatal heart attack. Anne, who worked tirelessly to help convict Kraven, can now concentrate on helping her husband recover. However, a new serial killer surfaces who curiously uses many of Kraven's techniques, and this maniac starts entering Anne's home and leaving her notes. But who could be using killing methods only the dead Kraven could know about, and why is Anne's husband acting so strangely?

Shelley, Mary. *Frankenstein.* 1818.

See chapter 3, "The Classics."

Simmons, Dan. *Song of Kali.* 1985.

An American poet visits his wife's native India with their young child. He is there on business, to pick up a poem cycle about the goddess Kali. However, once in Calcutta, the poet is nowhere to be found. This is a story about the evil of a place seeping into the very people who populate it. This work manages to be both scary and spiritual.

Stevenson, Robert Louis. *The Strange Case of Dr. Jekyll and Mr. Hyde.* 1886.

See chapter 3, "The Classics."

Strieber, Whitley. *Billy.* 1990.

Barton Royal is an evil, angry man searching to regain his lost childhood. In happy, twelve-year-old Billy Neary, Royal thinks he has found the perfect child. He kidnaps Billy. This terrifying novel is told from the points of view of both Royal and Billy.

Westlake, Donald. *The Ax.* 1997.

Burke Devore was laid off from his management position at a paper company and for two years has been trying to find another job. He decides to take matters into his own hands. Devore begins identifying his competition by placing fake ads in the trade journals and then kills off the prospective paper mill managers one by one.

9

Black Magic, Witches, Warlocks, and the Occult

Double, Double, Toil and Trouble

A person who practices occult arts may be called a witch, wizard, war-lock, sorcerer, magician, conjurer, shaman, magus, dream-weaver, soothsayer, healer, seer, or fortune-teller. Likewise, there is a huge body of literature written about these practitioners of magic, and no single motif is associated with them. Black-robed, stoop-shouldered hags coexist with New Age herbalists, Celtic druids, and fairy-tale and Disney depictions. Shakespeare's tempestuous witch sisters mesh with memories of *The Crucible* and *The Blair Witch Project,* and even the British wizard-in-training Harry Potter.

These prolific depictions of the witch/wizard mean different things to different people, but for hundreds of years witches have been associated with negative images. They use charms, potions, and curses. They are mischievous and bring ill fortune to others by inducing sickness, destroying crops, making cows go dry, ruining a batch of bread, or eating children. They belong to covens that hold sabbats under cover of darkness to discuss their magic and pay homage to their master, the Devil. In English and Scottish legends, witches possess the ability to fly on objects such as broomsticks and are supposed to have familiars or imps bestowed on them by the Devil when a witch bargains her soul away. These images are balanced by positive depictions of the white witch who uses her magical powers for good or to punish wicked people. In recent times, modern witches practicing the Wicca religion are said to have a deeper connection to the earth and nature that yields its practitioners special healing knowledge. However, the one uniform distinction of all witches is the element of magic. All have some sort of magical or mystic ability to manipulate the forces of nature.

Historically, it was not until the emergence of Christianity that magic makers were demonized and affiliated with Satan, culminating in the real-life horrors of the witch hunts and trials of the fifteenth to eighteenth centuries. It was commonly believed that Satan tempted individuals of weak faith and the easily corruptible (usually women) into entering a binding contract that gave them magical abilities or the chance to achieve worldly ambitions at the price of eternal damnation. The practice of witchcraft became associated with the ultimate evil, worship of the Devil, and thus it became a threat to the Christian church.

Witches and witchcraft cross all genres, but Anne Rice's Mayfair witches have found the greatest influence on this subgenre of horror. Starting with *The Witching Hour*, Rice introduced us to the multi-generational family of witches living in the Garden District of New Orleans. The Mayfair Witch Series traces the family from 7000 B.C. until the 1990s. With strong ties to the gothic tradition, Rice's witches, and much of modern witch horror, bear little resemblance to the Wicked Witch of the West or the Puritan witches of New England, but consist of powerful ancients passing their art down through their lineage to descendants coming to terms with their magical abilities. The witches in modern literature may not be bent on the obliteration or tormenting of man, but they are often flawed characters who can never be part of the dominant society of bustling computers and mundane life because they are not influenced by Christian morality or mainstream cultural conventions. What Rice does best is give her readers an alternative perspective on history through her witch characters' oppositional views and experiences.

Barry, Jonathan. *Cat Magic.* 1986.

> The witches in Maywell, New Jersey, peacefully coexisted with its Christian residents until the artist Amanda Walker comes to illustrate Constance Collier's next book and the radical Brother Simon arrives bent on destroying the witches.

Buchan, John. *Witch Wood.* 1927.

> Set in the seventeenth century, a young minister returns to the town

in which he was born, where he discovers a coven of devil worshipers while falling in love with one of their victims.

Card, Orson Scott. *Treasure Box.* 1996.

Millionaire computer software creator Quentin Fears was traumatized by his sister's childhood death. For years he lives as a recluse until he meets Madeleine Cryer, marries her, and then meets her strange family. Unfortunately, Madeleine is a succubus conjured by a witch, and Quentin must discover who the witch is and why she wants him to open a mysterious box.

Curtis, Peter. *The Devil's Own.* 1960.

In 1959 the 44-year-old spinster Deborah Mayfield becomes Walwyk's new headmistress. When frightening events begin to occur, she begins to suspect her new life was too good to be true.

Devlin, Serena. *The Red Witch.* 2000.

After pirate Jamie O'Roarke is freed from the oak tree that imprisoned him for 300 years, he tricks modern-day white witch Rebecca Love back to 1695 Salem, where she is denounced as a witch. She must escape her captivity in order to break the age-old curse and return to her home in the future.

Earhart, Rose.
Salem's Ghosts. 1998.

Mary English, a victim of the seventeenth-century Salem hysteria, was hung as a witch in 1692. Now her ghost has returned to the twentieth century to assist one of her descendants, Nora English, who is threatened by a man possessed by the ghost of George Corwin, a witch accuser of Mary's time. Together the ghosts of Salem band together to confront George Corwin and the Devil himself in order to free Salem of its centuries-old curse.

Dorcas Good: The Diary of a Salem Witch. 2000.

At age four, Dorcas Good and her mother are imprisoned after being accused of witchcraft during the Salem witch trials of 1692. In diary format, Dorcas retells how her father abused her and her mother, denounced his wife as a witch, and then sold Dorcas into a life of prostitution.

Goshgarian, Gary. *The Stone Circle*. 1997.

Widowed Peter Van Zandt, an archeology professor at a school in Boston, supervises an excavation on an island in Boston Harbor that uncovers stones reminiscent of Stonehenge. But these stones seem to be responsible for the disturbing visions of his dead wife beckoning him to join her that are threatening his sanity.

Hawkes, Judith. *A Heart of a Witch*. 1999.

In the small town of Green Hollow, New York, during the 1950s, twins Shelly and Kip Davies discover a coven of witches who have taken up residence in the Victorian inn situated across the street from their home. After losing two of their thirteen members, the coven asks the twins to join their ranks. During their apprenticeship, evil forces are unearthed and the coven must band together to battle this ominous danger.

Joyce, Graham. *Dark Sister*. 2000.

Maggie finds a witch's diary hidden in her home's old fireplace. With it she gains knowledge of her own powers as well as unleashing the Dark Sister, a malevolent force threatening her sanity and her family's well being.

Kimbriel, Katherine Elisha.
Night Calls. 1996.

Alfreda, a young girl growing up in an early nineteenth-century America full of myth and magic, is forced to accept her Gift and takes up arduous magical training in order to save the children of her village from being preyed upon by a band of werewolves.

Kindred Rites. 1997.

Thirteen-year-old Alfreda Sorensson, an apprentice in the Wise Arts, is kidnapped by a clan of sorcerers and is intended for their leader, a strange man known as the Keeper of Souls. (Sequel to *Night Calls*.)

Leiber, Fritz. *Conjure Wife*. 1993.

Norman Sayor, a professor of sociology, discovers that his wife Tansy practices witchcraft to ward off ill luck and evil influences. When Norman demands that Tansy quit sorcery, their lives fall apart and he is forced to put his prejudices aside and learn the skills of conjuring magic.

Maugham, W. Somerset. *The Magician.* 1908.

A young surgeon struggles against the wealthy and sinister Oliver Haddo, a practitioner of black magic, who has a perverse attraction to the doctor's beautiful fiancé.

Michaels, Barbara. *Other Worlds.* 1999.

Historical and fictitious crime experts, including the illusion expert Harry Houdini and the famous sleuth Sir Arthur Conan Doyle, explore two true cases of witchcraft and haunting in American history. The first is the early nineteenth-century legend of the Bell family who were haunted by ghosts for years, and the second is the haunting of the Phelps family in Connecticut in 1850. After each retelling the "experts" theorize and analyze the occult merits of the cases in order to determine their validity.

Passarella, J. G. *Wither.* 1999.

About 300 years ago, three women were hanged as witches in Windale, Massachusetts, as part of the witch hunts that swept through New England. Wendy Ward performs a ritual in the 1990s that goes awry, unwittingly freeing the three witches. Wendy must reverse what she has started before she is drawn into the evil.

Preiss, Byron, ed. *The Ultimate Witch.* 1993.

This collection of twenty-five short stories deals with witches and the art of witchcraft. Big-name contributors include Anne Rice, Dean Koontz, Tanith Lee, S. P. Somtow, and Ray Bradbury.

RavenWolf, Silver. *Beneath a Mountain Moon.* 1995.

With a long magical heritage of Scottish-Irish witchcraft, Elizabeyta Belladonna finds herself falling in forbidden love with a Christian minister. Together they try to solve the mystery of her grandmother's death and fight the dark powers of Jason Blackthorn and his Dark Men.

RICE, ANNE. MAYFAIR WITCHES

The Witching Hour. 1990.

Rowan Mayfair returns to New Orleans for her mother's funeral only to discover her family's shocking history, which spans four centuries of Mayfair witches, and the powerful influence and connection the family has to a spirit named Lasher.

Lasher. 1993.

Rowan Mayfair, queen of a coven of witches, flees the compelling, irresistible Lasher, who attempts to create a child strong enough for his spirit to inhabit.

Taltos: Lives of the Mayfair Witches. 1994.

Ahslar, a member of a giant humanlike race, teams up with the Mayfair witches to thwart whoever is killing their mutual friends.

Merrick. 2000.

See chapter 6, "Vampires."

Saul, John. *The Unwanted.* 1987.

After her mother is killed in a horrific accident, sixteen-year-old Cassie moves to False Harbor on Cape Cod to live with her father, whom she barely knows, and his family. There she discovers the dark secret of her birth and the terrifying powers of her gift.

Straub, Peter. *Shadowland.* 1981.

Sharing an interest in magic, Tom Flanagan and Del Nightingale, two freshmen at a boys school, form a friendship, become apprentices to a master magician, and then enter an alternative world where an ancient evil is responsible for horrible occurrences back at the boys school.

Urbancik, John. *A Game of Colors.* 2001.

This novella explores the occult through the eyes of Sara, a young girl determined to find her sister who has mysteriously disappeared. Tracing her sister's last steps, Sara joins a coven of witches and undergoes rigorous training, for the consequence of failure is death.

10

Demonic Possession and Satanism

The Devil Inside

Satan, Lucifer, Beelzebub; whatever we choose to call him, the Devil is a universal symbol of evil throughout Western culture. Therefore, it is not surprising that stories which revolve around the Prince of Darkness make up an entire subgenre of horror literature. Any time the Devil is invoked in a story, people become frightened and brace themselves for horrible things to start happening. This gut instinct on the reader's part makes it easy for the horror author to create an atmosphere of terror around a tale of demonic possession or satanism. But because stories of people selling their soul to the Devil or children being possessed are fairly common, the author also has to go out of his way to make his work fresh and original. As a result, the best novels within this subgenre not only deal with the Devil but also force the protagonist (and by extension the reader) to take a long hard look at himself and his own failings.

There are four basic plots or story lines one can find in these works: demonic possession, satanic ritual, the curse or cursed object, and of course, the selling of one's soul to the Devil. Each basic plot has its own characteristics, but the appeal factors for the subgenre remain the same. Moreover, some of the best books in this subgenre, like Karen Lynne Hall's *Dark Debts,* combine elements of all four story lines.

In the first story line, that of demonic possession, a person, usually an innocent child, is possessed by the Devil himself, one of his disciples, or an extremely evil person. Although any novel which explores issues revolving around Satan has an underlying religious element, possession tales tend to tackle this religious element in a much more direct manner. Priests and clergymen are common characters as they assist in exorcising the demon from the possessed. However, these representatives of organized religion are not always seen in the best light, as authors commonly use the demonic possession tale to satirize the clergy. The most important work in this subset is *The Exorcist* by William Peter Blatty. *The Exorcist* has become the modern standard for all possession tales. It is a testament to Blatty's imagination and writing skill that despite over twenty years distance, numerous showings of the movie version, and countless imitators, this novel has not turned into a cliché itself.

The next plot found within this subgenre involves satanic rituals and devil worship. These books revolve around characters who either conjure up the Devil or stumble upon a demon accidentally. Either way, at some point these characters make the decision to use the demonic powers to engage in evil of their own. Clive Barker, a horror master in general, has a knack for creating compelling tales of satanic rituals. His book *The Hellbound Heart* has terrified millions of readers and inspired the successful *Hellraiser* movie franchise. *The Hellbound Heart* accurately represents this subset in its tale of a man who, in greedily trying to summon a god of pleasure, instead unleashes the Cenobites, who are demons of torture. Brian Scott Smith's *When Shadows Fall* also provides a good illustration of the trouble caused by active devil worshipers.

The third plot found here is the tale of the curse or cursed object. In these works, someone with occult powers either curses a person who has wronged him or her or, more commonly, curses an object, leaving it behind to terrorize the next person who finds it. While the cursed person normally deserves what is coming to him, as we see in *Thinner* by Stephen King's alter ego, Richard Bachman, the cursed object normally inflicts its harm upon the obviously innocent. Although stories about cursed objects initially appear to belong in the subgenre containing black magic, upon closer examination they actually have more in common with tales of the Devil. Objects like the doll in Abigail McDaniels's *Althea* or the ring in *Death Stone* by Ruby Jean Jensen are more than simply infused with evil; they are quite literally possessed by it. That demonic power is then transferred to the owner of said object, or else the cursed object simply destroys all who come into contact with it. Also, because it is often the innocent such as Carol and her kids in *Althea* and Greta in *Death Stone* who find the cursed objects, these stories share a common characteristic with the demonic possession tales in this subgenre.

The final plot is probably the most familiar one: tales of those who sell their soul to the Devil. The plot follows the same structure every time: the character has a wish of some sort; the Devil appears to him offering all he can desire for the price of his everlasting soul; the character debates the deal for a bit and decides that his enjoyment of his worldly life is worth the sacrifice once he dies; and finally, the Devil comes calling for payment much earlier than the character expected or desired. Mythologies from cultures around the world have examples of these tales; classic literary works and operas have been built around this central conflict; and even American folklore contains well-known examples of those who have sold their souls to the Devil. It is the universal and timeless appeal of getting all you could dream of for nothing (in this life, at least) that keeps this story type fresh. It is a tempting offer that many a character has taken, from Goethe's Faust up to the present.

It is important that you be familiar with two works in this subgenre, *Rosemary's Baby* by Ira Levin and *The Monk* by Matthew Lewis. Levin's story of a man who arranges for his wife to be impregnated by the Devil so that he can become a famous actor is a classic work of horror. Because of the well-known movie, patrons will be familiar with the story and will quite often request it or a similar book. *The Monk* was originally published in 1796, almost two centuries before *Rosemary's Baby,* but it should not be overlooked by today's reader. Lewis's gothic tale recounts the exploits of a priest whose lust for a young girl ends up getting him condemned to death. He decides to sell his soul to the Devil in order to spare his life. Because *The Monk* has experienced a recent surge in popularity, with both Penguin Classics and the Oxford University Press releasing new editions within the last five years, and popular authors like Stephen King asserting its importance in the horror canon, you should be aware of this work.

While the plots of the novels in this subgenre may vary, their appeal factors are fairly similar. Obviously, all of the works play off of our fascination with the Devil and life after death in general. Our fear of demons, and the action that ensues once they are unleashed, is also responsible for attracting many readers to these satanic tales. However, it is the religious aspect, either blatant or implied, within these texts that is its largest appeal factor. Interestingly, it is not a single religion that is projected through these works, except for those books where a priest comes to exorcise a demon. It is a more general moral tone that permeates these stories. They ask us to ponder, even if only subconsciously, our own evil ways, while also reaffirming our decision to stay on the "right track." These stories also reinforce the hard work we do every day in order to attain our goals and make our lives better, by illustrating that you cannot get something for nothing. It is all too easy to succumb to evil in this world, as the works in this subgenre constantly remind us, and the price of following the Devil may not be worth it.

Bachman, Richard. *Thinner.* 1984.

In this, Stephen King's best-known work writing as Bachman, an overweight attorney accidentally kills a gypsy woman. Although he manages to wrangle himself out of a legal conviction, the gypsy's husband places a curse on him, causing the attorney to continuously lose weight.

Barker, Clive. *The Hellbound Heart.* 1986.

Frank is bored with what life has to offer, so he tries to summon a god of pleasure. But instead he accidentally calls up the Cenobites, demons of torture. This is the work that launched the highly profitable *Hellraiser* movie franchise. *Damnation Game* (1987) and *Everville* (1994) are also good suggestions for this subgenre, but be warned, Barker tends to be graphic in his depictions of both sex and violence.

Blatty, William Peter. *The Exorcist.* 1971.

The quintessential possession tale, *The Exorcist* is the novelization of a "true" story of the possession of a young girl in the 1940s. When eleven-year-old Reagan is possessed by an ancient demon, a group of adults assemble to save her. *The Exorcist* is still raw and powerful over thirty years later.

Blaylock, James P. *All the Bells on Earth.* 1995.

Walt Stebbins is your average entrepreneur in your typical small town. However, one day he receives a box meant for his archenemy, Robert Argyle. Inside is a pickled bluebird of happiness, promising to grant any wish. When Walt decides to keep the bird and pass on the empty package, he unknowingly begins battling the Devil.

Campbell, Ramsey. *The Influence*. 1988.

Queenie, a British spinster, has terrorized her family for years. With her death comes a well-earned respite from her horrible reign, or does it? It soon becomes apparent that Queenie cannot rest until she has inflicted more damage upon the family, as her spirit possesses a friend of the family. Also try *Ancient Images* (1989).

Farris, John. *Son of the Endless Night*. 1985.

Possessed by an evil demon, a young man commits a horrible murder. While at trial, the demon will do anything to prove his existence, including gruesomely stopping anyone who gets in his way. This book will appeal to those who enjoy courtroom dramas, although with a supernatural twist.

Farrow, David. *The Root of All Evil*. 1997.

Mystery writer David Farrow competently moves into horror with this demonic whodunit set in Charleston, South Carolina. A mystical ceremony, a craggy root, and a stormy night thirty years ago seem to have combined to allow the Devil's power to transfer from father to son. Now this powerful evil may be behind a series of murders.

Gray, Muriel. *The Trickster*. 1994.

Sam Hunt, a former shaman in training, has become disillusioned with his people and has dissociated himself from his heritage. However, he begins to have unexplained blackouts around the same time a series of murders is committed in his small Canadian town. Once Hunt realizes that he is being possessed by an evil Indian spirit, he must reconnect with his heritage in order to save the community and himself.

Hall, Karen Lynne. *Dark Debts*. 1996.

A cursed family is paying the price for its patriarch's satanism with their lives. Randa Phillips is called to identify one of these victims, her former lover, Cameron Landry; she thus begins a journey to take the remaining family members out of the Devil's hands. A large cast of characters with problems of their own is required to help free the Landrys.

Holder, Nancy. *Dead in the Water.* 1994.

A demonically possessed cruise boat skipper, Captain Reade, is making his passengers' life a living hell. The reader is along for a terrifying ride as passengers and crew members are forced to live out frighteningly realistic nightmares. This novel will haunt the reader long after the last page is read. Holder won a Bram Stoker Award for this work.

Jensen, Ruby Jean. *Death Stone.* 1989.

Greta is out playing when she discovers a skeleton and a ring in an abandoned well. After placing the ring on her finger, Greta is possessed by an evil force that wants her to kill her family.

King, Stephen. *Christine.* 1983.

Arnie Cunningham, a misfit teenager, buys a broken-down 1958 Plymouth Fury, but very soon he is obsessed with the car and possessed by its previous owner. *Needful Things* (1991) is also a good bet in this subgenre.

Koontz, Dean. *Cold Fire.* 1991.

Imagine you can foresee people's deaths and intervene to change their fate. Jim Ironheart has had this gift for most of his life. After witnessing his powers in action, Holly Thorne, a newspaper reporter, devotes herself to understanding Jim and helping him overcome the personal demons his powers invoke. Other demonic titles by Koontz include *Hideaway* (1992) and *The Mask* (1988).

Levin, Ira.

Rosemary's Baby. 1967.

See chapter 3, "The Classics."

Son of Rosemary. 1997.

This book is a sequel to *Rosemary's Baby.* In 1999 Rosemary Woodhouse awakens from a twenty-seven-year coma to find that her son, Andy, now thirty-three years old, is a spiritual leader thought to be the twenty-first century's savior. Disturbingly, however, Rosemary recognizes from his childhood that Andy's eyes occasionally take on a satanic cast, and she realizes a battle between good and evil is on the horizon with the fate of humanity in the balance.

Lewis, Matthew. *The Monk.* 1796.

 See chapter 3, "The Classics."

Lumley, Brian. *Demogorgon.* 1987.

 Charlie Trace is a thief who has been involved in his fair share of evil plots, yet he still seems to come out on top. However, when Trace gets mixed up with the Demogorgon, a disciple of Satan, who has been sent to Earth in a human form, he may finally be in over his head.

McDaniels, Abigail. *Althea.* 1995.

 Carol Lawson and her two daughters move into an inherited home in the bayous of Louisiana. Carol has an uneasy feeling about the old house, and when her daughter finds a strange doll in the home, Carol's suspicions become a terrifying reality.

Michaels, Barbara. *The Dark on the Other Side.* 1988.

 Michael Collins is intrigued with Linda Randolph. She is beautiful, wealthy, has a beautiful home, and an adoring, successful husband in author Gordon Randolph. Why then is she so frightened? As Collins researches Gordon's past, he comes to suspect the successful author of forming an alliance with dark forces and discovers that Linda's sanity may be a casualty of Gordon's bargain.

Mitchell, Mary Ann. *Drawn to the Grave.* 1997.

 Beverly falls in love with Carl only to realize that he is using her to cure himself of a terminal illness by slowly taking her life. Beverly devises a plan to save herself, hoping and praying that Carl's next victim, Meg, can stop the cycle.

Newman, Kim. *The Quorum.* 1994.

 Three friends are offered a deal with the Devil to ensure their success in the British media world. However, the price for this deal is the suffering of their mutual friend, Neil. They accept, but try to keep tabs on Neil's suffering and help him out as best they can. When the three hire a detective to help them watch Neil, the detective gets suspicious and their original deal starts to fall apart. Newman is a well-known British satirist and horror writer.

Powers, Tim. *Last Call.* 1992.

Set in Las Vegas, Scott Crane is playing against his father in a weird poker game using Tarot cards called Assumption. The stakes are high; they are playing for Scott's soul.

Reaves, Michael. *Voodoo Child.* 1998.

Set in New Orleans during the Mardi Gras celebration, Haitian sorcerer and drug lord Mal Sangre is preparing human sacrifices for the evil forces from a world beyond. Shane LaFitte, a voodoo priest, and Louisiana parole officer Lia St. Charles are reluctantly drawn into a good versus evil voodoo showdown.

Saperstein, David. *Red Devil.* 1989.

For years, Valarian has been behind much of the terror in the Soviet government, but who is he? Those who have figured out his connection to Satan himself have already been killed, but Washington and Moscow join forces for one last attempt at deposing the evil Valarian. This book is a good example of political horror.

Smith, Brian Scott. *When Shadows Fall.* 1997.

When Martin's aunt dies under suspicious circumstances, he is determined to learn the truth. His investigation leads him to witness a satanic ritual in the home of his aunt's friends. But his presence did not go undetected. Now Martin must elude them or die.

Smith, Guy. *The Dark One.* 1995.

Marcel's parents are going away and the Gorlays graciously agree to watch the young boy. The Gorlays enjoy the sweet child's company and begin to question the gossip they have heard about the boy's association with devil worship. But then their dog dies and an evil force descends upon their home. Could the rumors be true?

Strieber, Whitley. *Unholy Fire.* 1992.

Father John Rafferty is questioning his vow of celibacy as he is seduced by a young parishioner. At the same time, a demon has taken over the soul of a priest, beginning a gruesome killing spree. Father John must confront his own faith, controversy, and evil itself. *The Night Church* (1983) is also in this subgenre.

Wilson, F. Paul. *Nightworld.* 1993.

> Satan has brought long nights to New York, turning his demons loose upon the citizens under the cover of darkness. Humanity's only hope lies in the hands of an aging warrior, Glaeken, who has battled Satan many times across time and space. However, Glaeken is too weak to go after Satan alone and must gather up a band of warriors to assist him. Will they be strong enough to defeat the Devil?

11

Scientific and Biomedical Horror

The Doctor Will See You Now

Evil doctors, scientists out to control the world, deadly diseases, and government conspiracies inhabit the world of scientific and biomedical horror. While most of these works tend to read more like thrillers than like traditional horror works such as vampire tales or ghost stories, they are still extremely frightening. Writers in this subgenre like Robin Cook, Michael Crichton, and the master, Dean Koontz, have scared the pants off the public with their tales of science, disease, and doctors gone awry. But the subgenre has much deeper roots than these perennial best sellers imply. Its inception was marked by the publication of Mary Shelley's masterpiece *Frankenstein* in 1818. This well-known tale of a scientist's quest to create human life in his laboratory not only signaled the beginning of techno-horror, but many historians also cite it as the first true horror novel, period. Shelley planted the seed for a new type of literature: novels that question man's desire to conquer nature with science; and authors like the ones included here built upon her basic themes, incorporating a never-ending series of scientific discoveries in their books. The result is a seemingly infinite supply of science-based horror.

The basic characteristics of the works in this subgenre are easy to identify. First, they combine our obsession with technology with our fear of the Pandora's box which any new discoveries might open. In these novels, science—normally an objective and rational discipline—spawns terrifying and chaotic situations in which doctors experiment on unknowing patients, genetic clones run amok, biological weapons are released, computers begin to act with minds of their own, and deadly viruses wipe out humanity. These books mix tangible technology and known scientific principles with a bit of science fiction. The natural forces and technology we attempt to create and control slip from our tenuous grasp in these works. Sometimes a scientist sets out to control or destroy humanity for his own evil purposes; in other instances a deadly virus is mistakenly released; but in more cases than not, these works deal with an overzealous researcher who is obsessed with his work. This single-mindedness leads to disaster when the research takes on a life of its own. *Donovan's Brain* by Curt Siodmak is a perfect example of this characteristic. Here a scientist's obsession with creating a mechanism for allowing a human brain to live outside of the body succeeds too well, and the brain begins to control him.

The second characteristic of these works is that the terror is generated by the evil deeds of people one would normally trust and respect. Doctors, scientists, and the government use their power for nefarious purposes. Although people are generally a bit wary of scientists and the government wielding their power in evil ways, it is the tales of evil physicians that are always the most frightening ones in this subgenre. Doctors take the Hippocratic oath to "first do no harm," yet the medical professionals in the novels of Robin Cook, Michael Palmer, and Steven Spruill are always up to no good. The works in this subgenre prey on the average reader's awe with those who create new technologies, make scientific or medical discoveries that cure diseases, or simply make our lives easier and happier through their hard work. We are then forced to question our respect for these people. As a result, these novels are all the more terrifying because we know we must continue to trust those in the scientific community if we hope to reap the benefits of their discoveries, even if trusting all of them means that one "mad scientist" could destroy us all.

The last characteristic of scientific and biomedical horror novels is the intervention of a layperson or an ostracized scientist in the story. Although a scientist or doctor has caused the unspeakable horrors, it usually takes a hero from outside the established scientific community to save the day. A nonscientist or an outsider from within the scientific community is able to identify the emerging danger and, hopefully, put an end to the horrors. Two good examples of this common theme are Peter James's *Twilight*, in which a journalist uncovers an evil doctor's obsession with life after death;

and Michael Palmer's *Natural Causes,* where a doctor who incorporates alternative medicine in her treatment of pregnant women must discover who is killing her patients. It is this characteristic which turns many of these novels into cautionary tales. They encourage us, the layperson, to keep those who would manipulate nature in check because the horrors they describe could in fact happen someday.

While there are many authors, such as Robin Cook, Michael Crichton, and Richard Preston, who customarily write novels in this subgenre, the undisputed king of scientific and biomedical horror is Dean Koontz. His works are generally characterized by science fiction elements, in which the hero must battle technology, government conspiracies, or a scientific experiment gone wrong, and sometimes all three at once. In the course of creating these techno-thrillers, Koontz also manages to create compelling characters, weave interesting subplots into the story, and describe the natural beauty of his home state of California. The two works chosen for annotation here were selected because they are widely regarded as his best novels and also happen to be his self-professed favorites. *Mr. Murder* delves into the problems of cloning with a twist, asking what would happen if you were cloned without your knowledge and then that clone set out to kill you. *Watchers* is less overtly scientific but just as compelling. In this masterful example of storytelling, a young man with extremely bad luck is in for the adventure of a lifetime, one which happens to involve super-intelligent animals. These novels are excellent representatives of the best this subgenre has to offer. Koontz is able to use our fear of technology, our trust in scientists, and our faith in the common man to create techno-thrillers that both terrify and satisfy. It is no wonder that he is one of today's best-selling authors. (For more information about Dean Koontz and his works, see the appendix, "The Big Three," which provides a brief biographical sketch and a list of works by and about the author.)

It is important that we understand why readers are drawn to works of scientific and biomedical horror. Among their many appeal factors are their believability, their use of our preexisting fear of technology, and the eerie parallels they draw with current events. These novels are read because they tackle issues on the public's mind like cloning and bioterrorism. Patrons who read these works enjoy the fact that what terrifies them on the page today could happen in the real world tomorrow. Readers know that scientific research is done in the name of progress, but they also understand that this research could be used by the wrong people for the wrong reasons. Those who enjoy this subgenre are also drawn to its similarities with other works within the broader classification of the "thriller." This point is important to remember when you are working with patrons who do not normally read horror books, but regularly enjoy legal thrillers, espionage thrillers, etc. Many novels in this subgenre have more in common with their thriller cousins than with more traditional horror works. Therefore, they provide the perfect point of entry to a new genre for your thriller readers who have already "read everything you have."

Finally, although our goal is to point readers in the direction of good horror novels, we urge you not to forget about nonfiction where patrons who enjoy scientific and biomedical horror are concerned. The novels we discuss here are only terrifying because of their basis in scientific reality; the same patrons who enjoy being scared by the "what if" factor of these novels may enjoy the "already happened" nature of the numerous nonfiction works that mirror this subgenre. Three compelling true stories that are sure to terrify are Richard Preston's *The Hot Zone*, C. J. Hunter's *Virus Hunter*, and Judith Miller, Stephen Engelberg, and William Broad's *Germs: Biological Weapons and America's Secret War.*

Brouwer, Sigmund. *Double Helix*. 1995.

> In the middle of the New Mexico desert, Peter Von Kless, a genetic scientist, is running "the Institute." Von Kless hides behind his high-profile relief work, while he is really conducting grotesque experiments on unsuspecting people. This overtly Christian novel exposes the "horrors" of DNA research and abortion.

Cook, Robin. *Mutation*. 1989.

> In this homage to Shelley's *Frankenstein,* Victor created his genius son VJ by genetically altering an embryo. By VJ's tenth birthday it has become clear that he is far from the perfect son Victor set out to create. Like most of Robin Cook's books, the plot is fast paced and easy to follow; however, there are many medical terms and biological formulas within the text. If you enjoy this title, *Harmful Intent* (1990), *Outbreak* (1987), and just about every other Cook novel are also good bets.

Crichton, Michael. *The Andromeda Strain*. 1969.

> In Crichton's debut novel, the U.S. government has been working on a way to collect and breed extraterrestrial bacteria for potential use as

biological weapons. But when one of their bacteria-collecting satellites crashes into the Arizona desert, people begin getting sick. Nobel Prize-winning doctor Jeremy Stone and his crew work to stop the disease from spreading all over the Earth.

David, James. *Fragments.* 1997.

Research psychologist Wes Martin tries to create a perfect human by combining the most remarkable fragments from the psyches of five idiot savants. Of course, things do not go as planned and a sixth fragment, the spirit of a murdered woman, is added to the mix. The wronged woman wants revenge and decides to begin exacting it upon the other fragments.

Ghosh, Amitav. *The Calcutta Chromosome.* 1995.

Day after day, Antar sits in front of a computer watching it sort information, until one day the computer comes across some data that it cannot categorize. This begins a string of events that leads Antar on a search for Murugan, a scientist who disappeared while looking for a cure for malaria. The thriller gains steam as Antar uncovers the Calcutta Chromosome, which allows bits of personality to shift from person to person.

Hecht, Daniel. *The Babel Effect.* 2001.

Ryan and Jess McCloud are husband and wife, owners of a think tank, and renowned scientists. Their newest research project works from the hypothesis that violence is a virus that can be "cured." Their experiments send them to death rows and war zones and ultimately lead to Jess's kidnapping. Ryan is forced to continue alone, following the clues from Jess's research in an attempt to locate her before she becomes a victim of violence herself.

James, Peter. *Twilight.* 1991.

British reporter Kate Hemingway manages to attend the private exhumation of a woman who appears to have been buried alive. Her investigation into this horrible mistake leads her to suspect the involvement of Harvey Swire, an anesthesiologist with an extremely unhealthy interest in the afterlife. A battle between the good reporter and the evil doctor is inevitable; however, the conflict resolves with a satisfying plot twist.

King, Stephen. *The Stand*. 1978.

When an extremely deadly flu virus wipes out 99 percent of the Earth's population, human society as we know it is immediately obliterated. Those few who have survived must now take sides in what becomes a classic battle of good versus evil. King had this novel reprinted in unabridged form in 1990 with 150,000 additional words. *Firestarter* (1981) is also a work in this subgenre.

Koontz, Dean.
Watchers. 1987.

Travis Cornell has lost everyone close to him: mom, dad, brother, wife, and even the nine other members of his ten-member Special Forces squad. In an attempt to raise his spirits, Travis travels to the Santa Ana foothills to hunt rattlesnakes. His trip leads him on an adventure involving super-intelligent animals, the National Security Agency, and contract killers; but it is this unexpected adventure that may finally turn Travis's bad luck around. Also try *Night Chills* (1983).

Mr. Murder. 1993.

Marty, a fairly successful mystery writer living in California, is unaware of the existence of Alfie, his genetic clone. Alfie has been engineered to be an assassin, and when he learns of Marty's existence, Alfie sets his murderous sights on his unknowing creator. *Twilight Eyes* (1985) is also in this genre.

Levin, Ira. *The Stepford Wives*. 1972.

Stepford, Connecticut, appears to be the perfect suburban community, but when Joanna and her family move there, she discovers the truth. All of the women in the community are nothing more than their husbands' slaves. Joanna tries to organize a women's group to help liberate the women of Stepford, but her effort may not be enough to counter the sinister plan at work in her town.

Matheson, Richard. *The Incredible Shrinking Man*. 1956.

In this classic novella, Matheson tells the story of everyman Scott Carey's mysterious shrinking. As one can imagine, Scott's size leads him to encounter many "horrors." This story is well written and refreshing, and even after all these years, the ending continues to surprise first-time readers.

Ouellette, Pierre. *The Third Pandemic.* 1996.

A large corporation plans to create a devastating disease and then work on its cure, hoping to make billions of dollars selling the drug once enough people have died from the bacteria. The germs get out too soon, however, and soon a plague descends upon the entire world. Elaine Wilks, who unknowingly worked on the project for the corporation, gathers an interesting group to help her get to the bottom of this disaster and save civilization.

Palmer, Michael. *Natural Causes.* 1994.

Dr. Sarah Baldwin's obstetric patients begin bleeding to death during labor, and she starts to question her use of an herbal prenatal supplement in their treatment. But the common link in these deaths is not that easily explained. There are many suspects to consider, including HMO representatives and Sarah's own ex-boyfriend. Palmer is a physician, and all of his novels fall within this subgenre.

Preston, Richard. *The Cobra Event.* 1997.

Alice Austen, of the Centers for Disease Control, is given the task of connecting two suspicious deaths in New York City. A homeless man and a private school girl have both died from what appeared to be a bad cold. However, upon closer examination it is discovered that both were killed by a virus that devastated their immune systems. This terrifying thriller exposes the horrors of bioterrorism. Preston is better known as the author of the best-selling *The Hot Zone,* a nonfiction account of the dangerous Ebola virus.

Saul, John. *Creature.* 1989.

Saul can spin terrifying tales in just about any horror subgenre, and *Creature* is no exception. The Tanner family is relocated to the company town of Silverdale. Everything is perfect: beautiful scenery, happy families, and a high school football team that wins every game. However, this perfection comes at a price, and the Tanners' son must pay it by visiting the football team's "clinic."

Shelley, Mary. *Frankenstein.* 1818.

See chapter 3, "The Classics."

Siodmak, Curt. *Donovan's Brain*. 1942.

Dr. Patrick Cory is a young researcher who is obsessed with trying to keep a human brain alive outside of the body. When a plane crashes near his remote lab, Cory takes the brain of Donovan, one of the doomed victims. Dr. Cory succeeds in keeping Donovan's brain "alive," but his efforts may be too successful, as Donovan's brain begins to fight for control of the doctor's body. This little-known yet highly influential work has been listed by Stephen King as one of his favorite horror novels.

Spruill, Steven. *My Soul to Take*. 1994.

Surgeon Suzannah Lord was part of a government research project that implanted microchips into the brains of patients with visual problems. After refusing to sleep with her boss, Lord is fired, but years later she learns of a strange side effect of her research: the chip allows the patients to see the future. Lord, her naval officer sister, a chip-bearing artist, and a reporter band together in an attempt to stop those who have begun to use their new clairvoyant powers for nefarious purposes.

Watkins, Graham. *Virus*. 1995.

Can spending too much time working on the computer kill you? It can if your computer has the virus Watkins describes in this inventive, thrilling, and extremely satisfying novel. Watkins takes the reader's fears of technology and illness and spins them into a realistic tale of terror.

Wells, H. G. *The Island of Doctor Moreau*. 1896.

A mad doctor performs cruel experiments on animals on a remote South Sea island, experiments that blur the line between man and beast. This is both a study of what makes humanity stand out from the rest of the animal kingdom and a bloody horror story.

Wilson, F. Paul. *Implant*. 1997.

Besides editing the work of others in this subgenre, Wilson serves up some medical terror of his own with *Implant*. Dr. Duncan Lathram is a successful plastic surgeon to the rich and famous, but when government officials close to Lathram begin dying, the doctor's assistant begins putting the evidence together and it appears to lead right back to the good doctor.

Wilson, F. Paul, ed. *Diagnosis Terminal: An Anthology of Medical Terror.* 1996.

Wilson, a physician and medical-horror writer, edited this collection of fourteen frightening tales of evil medicine. This anthology, which includes stories by Wilson, Chet Williamson, and Steven Spruill, serves as a perfect introduction to the subgenre.

12

Psychological Horror
Mental Mayhem

We all have our personal demons, and authors of psychological horror exploit this by amplifying the average person's demons to horrific proportions. Psychological horror frightens the reader without setting monsters loose on an unsuspecting town; instead, it expertly crafts a dark atmosphere in which the characters' own thoughts, fears, guilt, and emotional instability literally take over their physical world. Then, to make matters worse, these characters usually try to deny their recently surfaced thoughts, which of course causes even more terrible things to happen. The characters in these works are so abused, wracked with guilt, or confused that they cannot function normally. This tends to lead to their downfall as they become unstable or even crazy. Dreams, hallucinations, and blurring of the lines between the real and the imagined in the characters' heads are all common occurrences in these novels. Works of psychological horror keep the characters in their pages, and the readers turning them, constantly guessing. What is real? What is simply a figment of the imagination? It is within the confines of these basic questions that the horror itself is created. When the worst thoughts from the darkest corners of our psyches are pushed front and center, we don't need a zombie to rise out of the graveyard to make us run away screaming.

Psychological horror is the most subtle subgenre of horror fiction. It is unique in that one of its main characteristics is the absence of a physical threat in the traditional sense. The horror aspect of these novels, that is, the scare factor, has an internal impetus. The characters are haunted by horrific events which they have since internalized; for example, guilt, voices in their heads, or abuse they sustained in the past. In some cases, these personal demons stay encased in the character's head, slowly driving him or her crazy, but never actually surfacing as reality. Daphne du Maurier's *Rebecca* provides a perfect example of this characteristic. The new Mrs. de Winter in haunted by her deceased predecessor. She can barely manage to function without being affected negatively by the memory of Rebecca. There are no ghosts in this novel, however; Mrs. de Winter is terrorized by her own doubts and fears about replacing a seemingly beloved woman. In other works, these internalized horrors gain so much power over the character that they literally leap out of the person and wreak havoc on the physical world, as the memories of Spyder Baxter do in Caitlin Kiernan's *Silk*. The characters found within the world of psychological horror may be physically threatened in some manner, but that which stalks them is born from their own minds.

Since the terrifying events in these novels spring from the heads of the characters, authors must craft a terrifying exterior atmosphere to enhance the internalized horrors. In most horror novels, description and setting are key to creating the appropriate atmosphere, without which the horror loses some of its power. With psychological horror, if the author fails to create a convincingly dark and foreboding feeling throughout the work, the novel will fail to induce any fear. *The Blood Countess* by Andrei Codresu provides an excellent example of this characteristic. A reporter in the 1990s visits his ancestral home in Hungary, where he discovers the horrifying crimes of one of his ancestors, a sixteenth-century countess. It appears she killed young virgins to preserve her own youth. The impetus for the terrifying situation is the reporter's guilt, but Codresu intensifies the horror by recounting the countess's exploits in detail and setting the modern-day sections of the story in a tumultuous post-Communist Hungary. The use of explicit detail and a cleverly chosen and chaotic modern setting help to turn this into a truly terrifying work of psychological horror.

The works in this subgenre do not share many other characteristics besides those two already discussed. Because the horror springs from the minds of the characters, these stories can really be about anything. Any internalized thought or feeling which the author can turn into a terrifying situation will do. In order to understand the breadth of subject matter and the multitude of ways in which horror can be conveyed in these works, it is best to look at the father of psychological horror, Edgar Allan Poe. Poe is credited with being the first American horror writer. As the numerous collections of his short stories attest to, his specialty was the tale that keeps the reader looking over her shoulder, just waiting for something terrible to pop up out of the shadows and attack. However, these physical threats never materialize; it is all in the characters' and readers' heads. Take one of Poe's most famous stories, "The Tell-Tale Heart," as an example. A man kills another, but this is not the impetus of the horror. The murderer then cuts the dead man's body up into pieces and buries them under the floorboards. The murderer appears to have gotten away with his evil deed, until he imagines that he hears the dead man's heart beating through the floor. The beating intensifies, driving the murderer crazy, and forcing him to give himself up to the authorities.

As the tell-tale heart beats, it gives terrifying life to all of our unspoken fears and guilt. This story is not only a defining example of psychological horror but has also inspired many other writers to try their hand at similar works. There are those like Stephen Marlowe in his impressive *The Lighthouse at the End of the World* who pay literal homage to Poe, but most of the authors found here write works like Richard Matheson's *Now You See It,* which casts an implicit wink at the master. Every work listed here is a direct descendant of the new type of story Poe created; therefore, we recommend suggesting a collection of Poe's works to all of your psychological horror readers.

The works of Poe and all those he inspired have kept readers on the edge of their seats for more than a century. But why? Perhaps because psychological horror appeals to the horror reader who is looking for a more realistic terrifying situation. Although there are some fantasy elements in these works, the "monsters" spring from the psyches of human characters, so many readers find the stories more realistic and thus more horrifying. John Saul's *The Unloved* is a good example of the reality of psychological horror, as a family is physically attacked by their own secrets after the death of their matriarch. Readers also seem to be drawn to this subgenre's expertly drawn settings, heavy use of description, and dark atmosphere.

Readers are most drawn to psychological horror because of its ability to get inside of their own heads. While we read about the demons inside of a character's head, our own unspoken fears and guilt are dredged up to the surface. It is hard to imagine something more frightening than being forced to confront your own fears and insecurities. Psychological horror digs in the darkest corners of our minds, and as we turn each page, the terror that is unearthed turns personal. Like the unknowing citizens in Bentley Little's *The Mailman* whose pasts come back to haunt them through the U.S. mail, we readers are forced to take a long hard look at ourselves as we make our way through the novels in this subgenre.

And yet we would not continue to read works of psychological horror if all they did was drive us crazy. Rather, these novels allow us to confront and possibly resolve the fears, guilt, and emotional instability inside of ourselves. One of the biggest "lessons" we draw from works of psychological horror is the fact that your situation only gets worse if you suppress the demons in your head and continue to carry the guilt of past sins. Poe's heart under the floorboards only beats louder the more it is ignored. In *It* by Stephen King, several adults are forced to confront a horrible force from their childhood that they have suppressed from memory for almost thirty years. Psychological horror may terrify us by drawing out that which we have suppressed in ourselves, but it also reminds us that we can stop the horror by addressing our personal demons.

Andrews, V. C. *Flowers in the Attic.* 1979.

> After their father dies, four children are locked in their grandparents' attic with their mother's blessing. Forced to bear this psychological horror, the children cope as best they can. *Flowers in the Attic* and Andrews's subsequent works have been read by millions of adolescent and adult women. Please be warned, this novel contains instances of child abuse and incest.

Barker, Clive. *Sacrament.* 1996.

> When the openly gay nature photographer Will Rabjohns is nearly mauled to death by a polar bear, he falls into a coma filled with strange and dangerous visions from his childhood in England. After Will breaks out of the coma, he returns to his home in San Francisco, but his visions have changed him. Then Will's father is brutally attacked back in England, allowing Will to piece his dreams together and sending him on a journey to confront the horrors of his past.

Campbell, Ramsey. *Obsession*. 1995.

Four young friends receive a cryptic note promising to grant them a wish for the price of something "you do not value." After making their wishes, the children's story flashes forward twenty years. Now adults, the friends are all battling bad luck. It appears they are finally paying a steep price for their childhood folly.

Codresu, Andrei. *The Blood Countess*. 1995.

In this historically based work, the action alternates between the story of the sixteenth-century Hungarian countess Elizabeth Bathory, a woman said to have killed virgins so that she could preserve her youth by bathing in their blood, and her modern-day distant relative, a reporter visiting a tumultuous post-Communist Hungary in an attempt to understand the past and assuage his guilt for his family's part in Hungary's problems. The two stories do eventually merge in an impressive yet violent climax.

du Maurier, Daphne. *Rebecca*. 1938.

See chapter 3, "The Classics."

Due, Tanarive. *The Between*. 1995.

Hilton James's grandmother gives her life to save him from drowning when he is a young boy. Now an adult, James is successful and happy. But when his wife starts receiving death threats, James begins to have overwhelmingly realistic visions of what his life could have become.

Kiernan, Caitlin. *Silk*. 1998.

Spyder Baxter is haunted by the troubling details and memories of her childhood. The demons of her past have become so overwhelming that they have left Spyder's head and are literally coming out of the woodwork. *Silk* is graphic, troubling, and satisfyingly frightening.

King, Stephen. *It*. 1986.

Seven Maine teenagers discover the source of a series of murders. Twenty-seven years later they are drawn back to their hometown by the same nameless evil. Will It conquer them this time? *Insomnia* (1994) and *Gerald's Game* (1992) are also good examples of this sub-genre.

Koja, Kathe. *The Cipher.* 1991.

Nakota and Nicholas find a hole that will alter whatever one decides to place in it. When Nicholas accidentally puts his hand in the hole, his life is changed forever. *The Cipher* won Koja a Bram Stoker Award and has since become an underground sensation.

Koontz, Dean. *Strangers.* 1986.

Weird things are happening in the lives of Dominick, Ginger, Ernie, Father Cronin, and Jack. All five live in different parts of the country and have never met one another, but their individual quests to under-stand their strange new afflictions lead them all to the Tranquility Motel in Elko, Nevada. Some of Koontz's other psychological titles include *The Key to Midnight* (1989) and *The House of Thunder* (1992).

Krabbe, Tim. *The Vanishing.* 1993. (Originally published in The Netherlands in 1984.)

A young Dutch couple are on vacation when the woman goes to use the rest room in a store and never returns. Her boyfriend, Rex Hofman, becomes obsessed with finding out what happened to her. When he meets her kidnapper years later, Rex is offered the chance to have all of his questions answered, but only at a steep price.

Lessing, Doris. *The Fifth Child.* 1988.

A normal couple has a model life with a big home and four perfect children; that is, until their fifth child, Ben, is born. This novel is as much about Ben as it is about our own unspoken fears about life and society. *Ben, in the World* (2000) was Lessing's much-anticipated sequel to *The Fifth Child.*

Little, Bentley. *The Mailman.* 1991.

After the previous mailman commits suicide, a new letter carrier begins delivering the townspeople nothing but good news. However, his true evil is soon discovered as the citizens begin receiving such items as mail from dead friends and body parts. This novel is eerily realistic.

Marlowe, Stephen. *The Lighthouse at the End of the World.* 1995.

Part biography, part mystery, and part psychological thriller, this novel uses a few facts about Edgar Allan Poe's life to compose a unique story of Poe's search for a the story behind a magical stone shard. Characters from Poe's own writings come alive to help him in his quest. This work is an imaginative homage to the psychological master.

Matheson, Richard. *Now You See It.* 1995.

An incapacitated magician, Maximilian Delacourt, invites his friends and family to his home for one last magic show. Max treats his audience to a grand show, that is, until the magic takes control of itself.

Norman, Howard. *The Haunting of L.* 2002.

In 1920s Canada, a young photographer, Peter Duvett, takes a job as the assistant to a strange but brilliant artist, Vienna Linn. Linn happens to be famous for his pictures of deadly accidents, some of which he begins to arrange himself. Throw into the mix Linn's seductive wife, who sees the spirits of the dead in her husband's photographs, and you have a complicated yet compelling tale. This novel is the conclusion of a trilogy which began with *The Bird Artist* (1995) and *The Museum Guard* (1998), but it could be read first.

Partridge, Norman. *Slippin' into Darkness.* 1994.

Almost twenty years after graduating from high school, a former cheerleader turned prostitute kills herself. Her death sets off a chain of events which haunt those who knew her in high school. Set over the course of one full day, this book illustrates how the bad decisions we make in our youth can come back to hurt us in adulthood. *Slippin' into Darkness* was honored with a Bram Stoker Award.

Poe, Edgar Allan. *The Collected Tales of Edgar Allan Poe.* 1992.

See chapter 3, "The Classics."

Saul, John. *The Unloved.* 1988.

The Devereaux family mansion sits imposingly on an island off the coast of South Carolina. The home and the family are ruled by a terrible matriarch. When she summons her son Kevin home, he only comes because she is ill. However, after Kevin and his family arrive, Mrs. Devereaux dies. Her death then unleashes a torrent of horrible family secrets upon those who remain.

Straub, Peter. *Hellfire Club.* 1996.

Nora Chancel, terrorized by nightmares of her time spent as a combat nurse in Vietnam, is kidnapped by Dick Dart. Their story is then intertwined with a curious tale from 1938, when terrifying events came in the wake of the completion of a horror story by a local writers' colony. The two narratives merge at the novel's climax as Nora and Dick visit the site of the writers' colony. Straub has written a gripping tale of horror within horror.

Tryon, Thomas. *The Other.* 1971.

Although they are twins, Niles and Holland could not be more different. While Niles is friendly and outgoing, Holland is painfully shy and has a tendency to hide from others. They spend a good deal of their time on their New England farm playing a strange game with their grandmother. In "The Game," she tells them they can be whatever or whomever they are concentrating on at the time. The story gets creepier as a series of murders take place in their peaceful town and it appears that Holland is somehow connected to them.

Wilhelm, Kate. *The Good Children.* 1988.

The four McNair children have faced the stresses of moving, entering a new school, and making new friends numerous times, but when they move to Oregon their Dad, Will, promises that they will stay put for a while. However, soon after moving, Will dies in an accident, beginning a chain of terrible events that seem to mirror the same tribulations faced by the original settlers in the area.

13

Splatterpunk or Extreme Horror

Horror's Cutting Edge

Where King had taken horror to the very edge of the unspeakable, Barker and Somtow had taken it over. Where King had flinched away at the final moment (the ritual infanticide in *Salem's Lot*, for example, or autocannibalism in *Survivor Type*) Barker showed it in cold, clinical detail, peeling back the flesh to give you a better look at the bloody interior.

—Lawrence Pearson, "The Splatterpunk Files"

The newest of the horror subgenres, splatterpunk, or extreme horror, made its appearance in the late 1980s. Often sexually explicit, these are intense and graphically violent stories that evoke strong emotional responses. Breaking social and literary conventions, this subgenre uses excess to enhance the effect of monstrous acts and heighten the story's impact. "A genre that alternately craves and shuns acceptance, Splatterpunk is . . . an amalgam of slasher films, brooding metal/Goth-inspired rock, and basic naughtiness disguised as nihilism."[1] The authors of splatterpunk horror don't leave you at the door to imagine the horrors beyond; they throw open the door, give you a little shove, and in raw surgical detail describe the horrors within. You don't leave without a little blood on your own hands and a sense that you saw more than you intended.

Occasionally referred to as gross-out literature, splatterpunk is a style that crosses into all the other subgenres. The novel may feature zombies, vampires, or a haunted house, but it is the graphic depictions that categorize it as splatterpunk. The graphic violence, harsh language, and sexual descriptions make this subgenre less mainstream and more experimental, or cutting edge, with the potential to transcend and redefine the horror genre.

Barker, Clive.
The Damnation Game. 1985.
See chapter 5, "Mummies, Zombies, and Golems."

Books of Blood. 1998.
Originally published as six separate paperback collections, this compilation volume is a hefty 818 pages of dark, imaginative, visceral short stories.

Bischoff, David. *The Crow: Quoth the Crow.* 1998.
Horror writer William Blessing is obsessed with Edgar Allan Poe. Seeking revenge on the man who raped his wife and destroyed his life, William must walk through the doorway or portal of truth and discover Poe's final secret.

Brite, Poppy Z.
Lost Souls. 1992.
See chapter 6, "Vampires."

Drawing Blood. 1993.
Returning to Missing Mile, North Carolina, where his father murdered his mother, younger brother, and then himself, Trevor McGee realizes he must face his inner demons. Taking up residence in his childhood home, Trevor meets and falls in love with Zach Bosch. Together they confront Trevor's haunted past and the evil the house itself carries that threatens to torment and destroy its inhabitants.

Exquisite Corpse. 1995.
Escaping from prison for the murders of twenty-three young men, Andrew Compton flees to New Orleans and teams up with a playboy murderer, Jay Byrne. Together they plan to perfect the art of killing

with their sights on Young Tran, a gay Louisiana teen who unwittingly falls into their lair.

Campbell, Ramsey. *Silent Children.* 2000.

Psychotic Hector Willie is obsessed with children in a grossly twisted way. When Ian and his younger stepsister, Charlotte, disappear their parents are frantic, but they only have to look as far as next door, for Willie has the children in his "care."

Collins, Nancy. *Sunglasses after Dark.* 1989.

See chapter 6, "Vampires."

Connolly, John. *Every Dead Thing.* 1999.

New York cop Charlie "Bird" Parker left the field after his wife and child were murdered by a serial killer who uses surgical dissection on his live victims. Hunting for the killer known as the Traveling Man, Parker follows a trail that leads him into the world of organized crime and the dangerous underworld of serial predators.

Ellis, Bret Easton.
American Psycho. 1991.

Twenty-six-year-old Pat Bateman is young and successful living in Manhattan. Then, for no apparent reason, he systematically starts killing people around him. Commenting on a society that has become desensitized to human suffering, this first-person narrative from the killer's point of view is both chilling and horrifying.

Glamorama. 1999.

Womanizing model Victor Ward lives in the party-going, fashion-crazed world of New York City. Paid to find a missing girl in London by a mysterious man, Victor becomes unwittingly sucked into a horrifying world of murderous terrorists.

Garton, Ray.
Lot Lizards. 1991.

Trucker Bill Ketter picks up a prostitute working the truck stops, one of a type referred to as "lot lizards." This one, however, is a vampire and soon Bill is added to the ranks of the undead. After running into his ex-wife and teenage son, he finds himself in battle against the vampires and their leader to save his son from a similar fate.

Shackled. 1997.

Assigned to follow the story of a missing boy, reporter Bentley Noble teams up with a woman who claims to be in communication with Liberace's ghost. Their search draws them into California's underworld of sexual deviants and satanists.

Kiernan, Caitlin R. *Threshold.* 2001.

Paleontologist Chance Mathews is left bereft by the recent death of her grandparents and best friend. Then she runs into Dancy Flammarion, an albino teenager who insists she is being pursued by monsters. Digging into Dancy's story, Chance discovers fossil records of an ancient terror that shapes people's lives for its own dreadful purposes.

Lansdale, Joe. *Freezer Burn.* 1999.

After a bungled robbery of a local fireworks stand, Bill Roberts, who has been living with his dead mother in order to collect her pension checks, hides out in a traveling country freak show made up of a strange miscellany of characters that include Siamese twins, a dog man, and the show's star attraction, a mysterious ice man.

Masterton, Graham. *Trauma.* 2002.

Bonnie Winters runs a business cleaning up domestic crime scenes. When she begins finding caterpillars at all her sites, she discovers an ancient Aztec belief that the insect is used as a daytime disguise for Itzpapalott, a demon who drives people to kill their loved ones. It is up to Winters to figure out the connection between the murders and the legend.

Matheson, Richard. *Created by.* 1993.

Creating the television hit of his career, *The Mercenary,* Hollywood writer Alan White is experiencing unprecedented success. But when the screen's violence starts playing itself out in real life, Alan realizes he needs to cancel the show before it cancels him.

McCammon, Robert. *Mine.* 1990.

See chapter 8, "Maniacs and Other Monsters."

Sammon, Paul, ed.

Splatterpunks: Extreme Horror. 1990.

An anthology of splatterpunk writings from such authors as John

Skipp, Clive Barker, and Nancy Collins. This short story collection would be a good introduction to the writers of extreme horror.

Splatterpunks II: Over the Edge. 1995.

A second collection of splatterpunk short stories from some of the best-known authors of horror, including Clive Barker and Poppy Z. Brite. This is an updated assemblage of extreme horror.

Saul, John. *Black Lightning.* 1995.

See chapter 8, "Maniacs and Other Monsters."

Schow, David. *The Kill Riff.* 1988.

Seeking revenge for his daughter's death at a rock concert, Lucas Ellington is driven mad as he kills the members of the band, Whip Hand, that he blames for inciting the audience's stampede. Lead singer Gabriel Stannard is the last one alive and must stalk the stalker to stay alive.

Skipp, John, and Craig Spector. *The Light at the End.* 1986.

Cynical punk/Goth Rudy Pasko is turned into a vampire by an evil ancient entity that perpetuates a series of bizarre, brutal murders. Using his new powers, Rudy is acting out against the world he has always hated while Joseph Hunter, who vows to kill him, is only one step behind.

Slade, Michael.

Headhunter. 1984.

When the headless bodies of brutally murdered women turn up in Vancouver, British Columbia, the Royal Canadian Mounted Police led by commander Robert DeClerq are drawn into the mind of a peculiarly perverse psychopath. ("Michael Slade" is a pen name for Jay Clarke, John Banks, and Lee Clark.)

Ghoul. 1987.

Is there a connection between the Canadian Mountie Zinc Chandler's investigation of a rock group called Ghoul and Scotland Yard's search for a psychotic butcher dubbed the Vampire Killer? The answer lies in a dark and bloody trail through Canada, the United States, and England that Zinc must follow in order to stop this madman before he kills again.

Ripper. 1994.

The Royal Canadian Mounted Police investigate the serial murders that pattern *Jolly Rogers,* a thriller about to be published. As Mountie Robert DeClerq uses the novel to trace the motivations back to the demons that drove Jack the Ripper, he races against time to stop this vicious killer.

Primal Scream. 1998.

The Headhunter, a psychopath who left a trail of headless bodies for Canadian police eleven years earlier, is back, but this time he is stalking Mountie Robert DeClerq. DeClerq must save a young girl and himself before the Headhunter achieves his revenge.

Burnt Bones. 1999.

A madman calling himself Mephuisto buries his victims alive and then listens to their screams through a transmitter. Canadian Mountie Robert DeClerq and American detective Jenna Bond are lured into his games as they hunt for the kidnapped Nick Craven, a fellow Mountie and friend of DeClerq, in a race against the clock.

Death's Door. 2002.

Tying the theft of a mummy in England to the brutal murder of young runaways in Canada, Robert DeClerq and his team of investigators discover an underground porn ring and the very worst in human depravity.

Somtow, S. P. *Vampire Junction.* 1984.

See chapter 6, "Vampires."

Straub, Peter. *Floating Dragon.* 1983.

Hampstead, an affluent yuppie suburb, appears to be a nice place to live until it is besieged by unspeakable horror. Richard Allbee, Patsy McCloud, Graham Williams, and Tabby Smithfield must escape the town before they become victims of its malignancy.

Strieber, Whitley. *The Forbidden Zone.* 1993.

See chapter 7, "Werewolves and Animals of Terror."

NOTES

The epigraph for this chapter is from Lawrence Pearson, "The Splatterpunk Files," Stealth Press website, http://www.stealthpress.com.

1. Review of *Splatterpunks II: Over the Edge,* edited by Paul Sammon, *Kirkus Reviews* (July 1994).

14

Horror Resources
How to Hunt for the Haunted

One of the most common misconceptions that plagues librarians who help fiction readers is that they must have read a book in order to suggest it. But in reality, this would be analogous to forcing a reference librarian to read the entire *World Book Encyclopedia* from cover to cover. Just as the reference librarian turns to an encyclopedia, an almanac, or the Internet to begin to assist her patrons, the readers' advisor can choose from a wide range of reference sources to fill in the gaps in her personal knowledge. Of course, helping a reader to find "the perfect book" is a much more intimate experience than, for example, locating the average yearly rainfall in Guatemala; but that intimacy should not scare you away from using the same basic techniques of library science. One of these techniques is knowing exactly which reference sources would be the best ones to answer the question you have just received. Therefore, we present this chapter as a guide to the sources you can use to answer your readers' horror questions.

We will not attempt to identify each and every horror resource out there (that would be an entire book on its own). Instead, we will focus on the best and fastest places which the readers' advisor can turn to for answers and ideas. These sources have been selected for their ability to help you quickly answer the vast majority of the questions you will receive. However, we realize that if read in a vacuum, this chapter is not helpful to you. Therefore, we have arranged it in such a way that it will help you when you really need it—when you are in the trenches, answering a question for an impatient patron. We have broken up this chapter into the following sections: reference sources, print and electronic; magazines, print and electronic; and associations and awards.

Horror Reference Sources: Print and Electronic

NoveList

Experience has taught us that on the front lines of readers' advisory, after your catalog, the first line of defense for most questions is EBSCO's fiction database, NoveList. However, using NoveList for horror inquiries has both pros and cons; the trick is understanding which patrons and questions will benefit most from this wonderful resource. For any genre, NoveList is best used when you have no idea where to begin or as a continuing education resource. For example, NoveList is a great place to go to quickly as a patron is standing in front of you and still explaining his or her request. Let's say someone asks you for a book similar to Robin Cook's *Mutation*. If you have never read Cook's work and are not sure what type of books he writes, you should begin by doing a title search in NoveList. Right away you will get a short synopsis, a list of pertinent subject headings, and a link to a list of other "Medical Horror" novels. You could then go straight to that list; or you could ask the patron exactly what he or she liked about *Mutation*, click on "Choose Subject Headings," and then click on those terms which are most similar to what your patron liked about the novel. A list of books with those subject headings will then be generated for you. NoveList can also help you to become more familiar with a genre. You can click on "Explore Fiction," choose "Horror," and then peruse the various lists of subgenres. Finally, you can use the database's upgraded searching features to locate articles and interviews that pertain to horror interests. For instance, in October 2002, NoveList featured horror's hottest commodity of the moment, Neil Gaiman, by posting the work he did for *Booklist's* Halloween issue.

The preceding examples illustrate NoveList at its most helpful; however, NoveList's usefulness for horror readers does have its limits. Specifically, in the aforementioned lists of books under various horror subgenres, NoveList's offerings are uneven. A good example of this can be seen in its prepared list of only six "Haunted House" books, while it provides links to almost thirty "Medical Horror" novels. The haunted house is one of horror's most important subgenres, and though medical horror is worthy of its long list, haunted houses would need at least the same amount of attention in order for us to wholeheartedly endorse NoveList for your horror needs.

Basically, the use of NoveList boils down to a few simple rules of thumb. If you have absolutely no experience with horror fiction, use NoveList in your free time to become better acquainted with its subgenres, common subject headings, and major authors. Also use it when a patron needs an answer right away and you are simply at a loss to address his or her question. Finally, NoveList is perfect for helping you and your staff to produce annotated lists or displays quickly; the extensive fiction subject headings, plot descriptions, and reprinted reviews that accompany most titles are invaluable in this regard. However, if either you or the patron are well versed in horror, we recommend you use the other resources listed here first.

Hooked on Horror

While NoveList is great for the horror neophyte, if you are dealing with a patron who is a horror buff, you need to turn to the experts, Anthony Fonseca and June Michelle Pulliam. Their 1999 book *Hooked on Horror: A Guide to Reading Interests in Horror Fiction* is the most thorough reference work on horror fiction ever written.[1] *Hooked on Horror* not only impressed those in the readers' advisory field, but it also made *Library Journal's* prestigious list of the "Year's Best Reference Books" in 2000. What makes *Hooked on Horror* such a useful reference source is its perfect balance of organization and comprehensiveness. *Hooked on Horror* contains almost too much information; simply open this resource to any page and you will be deluged by facts, suggestions, and extensive lists. However, Fonseca and Pulliam manage to take all this useful information and make it immediately accessible by employing an easy-to-follow method of organization. The opening chapters define horror, highlight its appeal, recount a short history of the genre, and most importantly, explain exactly how the book should be used. Fonseca and Pulliam then provide fourteen chapters of subgenres with annotated lists. These lists include subject headings, read-a-likes, and spotlights on key works within the subgenre. Each chapter also includes an annotated list of important films in the category. Finally, each subgenre discussion ends with the authors' "picks"—lists of their favorite books and films in each category. The "picks" alone are worth the price of admission with this resource; we have turned to these lists when, for example, we must quickly suggest a good werewolf book to a patron. *Hooked on Horror* also includes information on nine notable horror writers, a ready reference chapter, publisher information, and an Internet guide. The table of contents and the three indexes (short story, subject, and author/title) of *Hooked on Horror* are extremely useful navigation tools, pointing either the librarian or the patron to the information they are seeking quickly.

The Year's Best Fantasy and Horror

Another one of our favorite print resources is the annual publication *The Year's Best Fantasy and Horror*. This series, edited by Ellen Datlow and Terri Windling, compiles the best short fiction, poems, and essays within the genres and publishes a new collection each summer. Although having access to the "best" horror for any given year is an important aspect of this resource, it is the introductory chapters that we recommend in this work. Each book begins with a recap of the year in fantasy and horror. For example, the "Summation 1999: Horror" in the thirteenth edition is thirty-five pages long and discusses book and magazine publishing news, notable novels, anthologies (including reprints), collections, and nonfiction works. There is also information on magazines, newsletters, illustrated works, and small press offerings with contact information. *The Year's Best Fantasy and Horror* may be less useful than *Hooked on Horror* for your everyday horror questions, but as a reference work for the readers' advisor this book is invaluable. We highly recommend getting your hands on a copy of this collection annually. Whether you buy it or acquire it by interlibrary loan, take some time to read the fifty or so pages of introductory material. By giving an hour of your time once a year, you can be assured of catching up on all the horror news of the past twelve months. Finally, this book is also a good bet to recommend to your hard-core horror fans.

www.horror.org

While *The Year's Best Fantasy and Horror* may recap everything you need to know about horror from the previous year, the question still remains, where should you turn to for the most current horror information? Thanks to the Internet, the answer is just a few clicks away. The reputable

Horror Writers Association, or HWA (see the "Horror Associations and Awards" section below), has compiled the most useful (to librarians at least) horror website at www.horror.org. There are literally thousands of horror-related websites on the Internet, and due to the erotic undertones of much of the genre, many of them are not appropriate for our line of work. Therefore, as the leading professional association in the genre, the HWA has taken it upon itself to unknot the tangled horror offerings on the Web. The site is neatly laid out with a navigation bar on the left which leads to lists of award-winning books, reading lists, and, thankfully, horror links. It is this final component which we recommend as a reference source. The HWA maintains and updates this directory of horror-related Internet sites and makes it available for free access. The links are broken up into various categories, including horror book publishers (large and small presses), booksellers, conventions, magazines (electronic and print), miscellaneous topics, and HWA regional chapters. There are almost too many links here, but thankfully, many are annotated, which helps immensely. This genre-specific web directory is the best we have come across, and as a result, we turn to it frequently both to answer questions or to pass on to one of our horror-loving patrons.

In February 2003 the HWA website added to its home page a special section for librarians (look under "Special Pages" on the left navigation column of the main page). This librarian-centric area has links to information on how the HWA can be of service to you. Detailed information about signing up for newsletters, joining the HWA, and arranging for a horror author to visit your library is all just a click away. There are also essays, the current month's new horror releases, and the HWA's list of the best horror novels of all time.

We feel the reference sources listed above constitute the bare minimum of resources you would need in order to answer most of your patrons' horror-related questions. If you have a personal interest in the genre, you should also look at *Fantasy and Horror,* edited by Neil Barron, and *St. James Guide to Horror, Ghost and Gothic Writers,* edited by David Pringle. Both of these works are well respected and extremely useful.

Horror Magazines: Print and Electronic

Librarians are seldom shocked by the daunting number of magazines available on just about any topic one could dream up, so it will come as no surprise that there are dozens of horror offerings in this category. The key is knowing which magazines are even worth a casual read, let alone the commitment of a subscription. To sort out the offerings in this category, we recommend using two of the reference sources detailed above. Both *Hooked on Horror* and the "Horror Links" section of the HWA's website will provide a prescreened list of magazines. However, for our purposes, we are going to highlight one magazine from each medium, print and electronic.

Weird Tales

If you could only read one horror magazine, there is no question that it should be *Weird Tales*. This magazine is an important part of the past and present of horror fiction, having published original stories by Robert Bloch, Ray Bradbury, Fritz Leiber, and C. L. Moore. *Weird Tales* also published Robert E. Howard's *Conan* stories and H. P. Lovecraft's Cthulhu Mythos tales. Not only has *Weird Tales* been an integral part of the history of horror literature, but its own history makes for a good tale itself. After a few false starts, *Weird Tales* was first published in March 1923 in Chicago by Jacob Clark Henneberger as an outlet for the writer of "unusual fiction" to "express his innermost feelings in a manner befitting great literature." *Weird Tales* suffered many financial crises in the ensuing years. To counter high production costs, the publishers were constantly changing the magazine's layout, size, and number of pages.[2] The editorial staff kept the magazine together until March 1954, after an original run of 279 issues. Then in 1998 *Weird Tales* officially resurfaced under the direction of DNA Publications, just in time to release a special seventy-fifth anniversary issue. The new *Weird Tales* has remained true to the old; it even began numbering the new issues from 279. Despite its persistent money problems and many reincarnations, *Weird Tales* has remained true to its original goal of "establishing a long-term market place for stories about the unusual and bizarre, [and] creating a haven where writers could let their imaginations soar."[3] If you are interested in delving further into the world of horror magazines, we also recommend taking a look at *Cemetery Dance, Dark Realms, Dreams of Decadence,* and *Talebones.*

Gothic.Net

While there is one obvious standard in the realm of print magazines, electronic horror magazines have not been around long enough for us to declare a clear front-runner. However, our favorite is *Gothic.Net* (www.gothic.net). *Gothic.Net* is the self-proclaimed longest-running webzine of horror fiction on the Internet. Entering its sixth year, *Gothic.Net* publishes "the latest, original, unpublished short fiction and articles by the best in horror." Although you can browse *Gothic.Net* for free, to use this magazine to its fullest you need to sign up for a subscription, or "membership," for fifteen dollars a year. What makes this electronic magazine superior to its counterparts on the Web is the fact that it takes itself seriously as a horror magazine. For example, the home page clearly lists the publication schedule: Monday, horror fiction; Tuesday, editorials; Wednesday, column (columnists are on a rotating schedule); Thursday, letters to the editor; and Friday, poetry. *Gothic.Net* also lists a schedule of upcoming pieces. This is especially useful if you or a patron is particularly interested in a specific author's newest work. *Gothic.Net* is also extremely easy to navigate. Once you have signed up and chosen a log-in and password, moving around the site, reading articles and fiction, and posting your own comments are extremely easy. For both quality of content and ease of use, we highly recommend subscribing to *Gothic.Net*. If you would like to look at a few more electronic magazines, try *Alien Online, Monsterzine.com* (dedicated to the monster movie genre), or *SciFi.com,* which has recently begun publishing fiction edited by Ellen Datlow (mentioned above as coeditor of *The Year's Best Fantasy and Horror*). All of their web addresses, along with further suggestions, can be accessed through the HWA's website at www.hwa.org/horrorlinks.htm.

Horror Associations and Awards

Horror novels and films have a rabid audience of fans, many of whom devote their time to creating and maintaining organizations that revolve around the genre. There are several well-respected, official horror associations which the librarian can turn to for well-documented advice, information, and most importantly, lists of award-winning books. These associations exist internationally and all over the United States; most even allow librarians to join their ranks. However, it is not necessary for the readers' advisor to join one of these associations in order to reap the benefits of their expertise. Simply by knowing who these groups are, accessing their websites or newsletters when necessary, and keeping an eye out for the announcement of their annual award winners, the readers' advisor can handle many of her patrons' horror queries with ease.

Horror Writers Association

As a readers' advisor it is imperative for you to be familiar with the Horror Writers Association (HWA). It proclaims itself as "a worldwide organization of writers and publishing professionals dedicated to promoting dark literature and the interests of those who write it." The HWA has an impressive and extremely useful website, www.horror.org (as detailed above), and the HWA also hands out the most prestigious awards for works of horror literature, the Bram Stoker Awards.

Any discussion of the HWA should begin with a history of the organization itself. As recounted on its website at www.horror.org/history.htm, the story of how the HWA became influential mirrors horror's own rise from pulp fiction to a more respectable genre. It all began back in 1984 when Robert McCammon, already the author of half a dozen horror novels, mentioned in a *Publisher's Weekly* interview how he longed for an association of horror writers similar to their science fiction and mystery counterparts. Not only would this organization help to legitimize horror as its own genre, but it would also give horror writers a place to turn to for advice and camaraderie. McCammon named his imagined association the Horror/Occult Writers League, or HOWL for short.

Surprisingly, McCammon's statements about HOWL aroused interest from a wide variety of people, as well as major media outlets and bookstore chains. People began contacting McCammon, asking to sign up for this still imaginary association. Faced with this enthusiastic response, McCammon set out to create his dream association. With the help of his friend, the author Joe Lansdale and Joe's wife, Karen, HOWL sent out letters of invitation to 177 writers. After 88 responded, the first horror writers' association was born.

However, like the genre it represents, HOWL was initially not taken seriously. First of all, the abbreviation HOWL incited ridicule at every turn, and second, the high-profile authors in the genre at the time, such as Stephen King and Peter Straub, were not interested in membership. But McCammon and his crew trudged along down the obstacle-strewn path to legitimacy. Their next attempt at professional acceptance came in November 1985 at the World Fantasy Convention, where they knew hundreds of horror writers would be gathered. While only twenty-four people attended the

HOWL meeting, the group did take the important step of changing the association's name to the more official-sounding "Horror Writers of America."

Armed with a new name, this small group of dedicated members began focusing on making the association more relevant to professional horror writers. In 1986 Dean Koontz was voted the association's first president, and in March 1987 the HWA was legally incorporated. With this last hurdle toward legitimacy cleared, horror writers, including King and Straub, began joining in droves. The HWA grew to include an international membership, so in 1993 the association changed its name to "Horror Writers Association" to reflect its new worldwide scope.

Today the Horror Writers Association has more than 1,000 members divided into four categories: lifetime, active, associate, and affiliate. Anyone who can demonstrate a serious interest in horror fiction is welcome to join the HWA as an affiliate member; this would include any readers' advisor. The benefits of membership include receiving the HWA's bimonthly newsletter, e-mail bulletins, passwords to the "Members Only" areas on its website, and access to its two electronic discussion lists, SFF-Net and Dueling Modems. However, for most readers' advisors, simply accessing the HWA's amazing website at www.horror.org will provide much of the horror information or answers you are looking for.

Besides fighting for horror legitimacy and compiling the most complete horror website on the Internet, the HWA is invaluable for its annual, highly respected Bram Stoker Awards. These awards are named for the horror master who created one of the best-known characters in fiction, Dracula. The Stoker Awards are handed out annually in twelve categories: novel, first novel, short fiction, long fiction, fiction collection, poetry collection, anthology, nonfiction, illustrated narrative, screenplay, work for young readers, and alternative forms. In order to limit competition between its members, the HWA makes sure to specify that these awards are not for the "year's best" works, but rather for "superior achievement." Any work of dark fiction written in English is eligible. The Bram Stoker Awards are nonjuried awards, much like the Oscars or Grammys. A first ballot is compiled based on recommendations and is presented to the active membership for their vote. The results are then compiled into a second ballot of nominees from which the eventual winners are chosen. "Lifetime Achievement" awards may also be presented. Past award winners include Neil Gaiman, Stephen King, John Shirley, and Peter Straub. *The Year's Best Fantasy and Horror* anthology is a perennial nominee and past winner. For a complete list of the 2002 Bram Stoker Award winners, see figure 14-1.

Novel: *The Night Class* by Tom Piccirilli

First Novel: *The Lovely Bones* by Alice Sebold

Long Fiction: (tie) *El Dia de los Muertos* by Brian A. Hopkins
          "My Work Is Not Yet Done" by Thomas Ligotti

Short Fiction: "The Misfit Child Grows Fat on Despair" by Tom Piccirilli

Fiction Collection: *One More for the Road* by Ray Bradbury

Anthology: *The Darker Side* edited by John Pelan

Nonfiction: *Ramsey Campbell, Probably* by Ramsey Campbell

Illustrated Narrative: *Nightside* (issues 1–4) by Robert Weinberg

Screenplay: *Frailty* by Brent Hanley

Work for Young Readers: *Coraline* by Neil Gaiman

Poetry Collection: *The Gossamer Eye* by Mark McLaughlin, Rain Graves, and
     David Niall Wilson

Alternative Forms: *Imagination Box* (multimedia CD) by Steve Tem and
     Melanie Tem

Lifetime Achievement Awards: Stephen King
          J. N. Willamson

For a complete list of all nominees and winners from 1987 to the present, go
to www.horror.org.

FIGURE 14-1   2002 Bram Stoker Award Winners

International Horror Guild Awards

While the Stoker Awards are nonjuried, the International Horror Guild (IHG) presents a juried alternative. Much like the National Book Awards or the Booker Prize for general fiction, the IHG Awards are chosen by a panel of well-established horror critics and reviewers. Created in 1995 to "recognize outstanding achievements in the field of Horror and Dark Fantasy," the International Horror Guild's sole purpose as an association is to present its award winners each year. Although winners are chosen by a jury, the IHG asks that the public nominate its favorite works by sending e-mails to the IHG's home page at www.ihgonline.org.

The IHG Award judges normally announce their final decisions during a special presentation at the World Horror Convention. The twelve award categories are for novel, first novel, long fiction, short fiction, collection, nonfiction, anthology, illustrated narrative, publication, art, film, and television. A "Living Legend" award is also often presented for lifetime achievement during the ceremony. A full list of award winners and nominees can be found at www.ihgonline.org/prevrec.html.

The HWA and the IHG are not the only horror associations out there, but because they are the only ones to issue internationally recognized prizes for horror writing, they are the most important to you as a readers' advisor. If you or your patrons are interested in other associations, especially ones that meet in your area, you can turn to the "Links" section of the HWA website for an extensive list of horror-related associations.

Our Recommendations

The resources described in this chapter will assist you with just about any horror inquiry on their own, and what makes them even more useful is their potential to lead you to thousands of other resources. However, we understand that money is tight and horror is only one of many genres you must address on a daily basis. Therefore, if you can only afford one of the resources mentioned above, we recommend Fonseca and Pulliam's *Hooked on Horror;* this comprehensive reference work is the best general source about horror fiction that we have encountered. We have used *Hooked on Horror* to answer more horror-related questions than any other tool, print or electronic. We also recommend that you keep the HWA website, www.horror.org, bookmarked for easy access. With the present volume and these two sources, you should be able to confidently tackle most horror-related questions. If you want to go a little further, acquire *The Year's Best Fantasy and Horror* and read the introductory material. We also recommend keeping a list of the most recent HWA and IHG award winners handy (much like the one in figure 14-1). Award winners make great suggestions in any genre.

Finally, we know from experience that you can have a fully stocked reference shelf, subscriptions to all the appropriate databases, and a familiarity with the actual novels in a genre and still get a question that appears unanswerable. For this we remind you to subscribe to the electronic discussion list Fiction-L.[4] When all hope is lost, through this list you can tap into the knowledge of readers' advisors from all over the country. Just send a question to the entire group, and the chances are very good that someone will either know the answer or point you in the direction of a resource that will provide the information your patron has requested. Fiction-L is an important reminder to us all that although we may be sitting alone at the service desk, we are part of a larger community of readers' advisors who love fiction.

NOTES

1. Just as this book was completed in 2003, Fonseca and Pulliam published a new edition of *Hooked on Horror*. We used it sparingly in writing this work.
2. For a more complete history of *Weird Tales*, see the official *Weird Tales* website at http://www.weird-tales.com/index.html. This site also includes a reprint of the magazine's 1924 editorial explaining the philosophy behind "weird tales."
3. Quoted from http://www.weird-tales.com/history.html.
4. See http://www.ebrary.org/rs/Flmenu.html for details about the discussion list and instructions on how to subscribe to it.

15

Collection Development
Cultivating the Seeds of Fear

Cultivating and maintaining any collection is a difficult task, and unfortunately, there are no set rules to help guide you. As a result, collection development is the most important professional duty we have as librarians. However, it might help to look at this task as a practiced art rather than a learned science. Collection development consists of both acquiring new materials for your collection and weeding out those works that are no longer relevant to your collection. It is in the act of identifying what should be purchased and what can be discarded that the librarian makes some of his or her most important professional decisions. What we decide to make available on our shelves affects our patrons more directly than most other decisions we make. So we would be remiss if we did not address collection development as it pertains to your horror collection.

One of the biggest mistakes librarians make when discussing collection development is the assumption that the process is comprised of only one part: acquiring new materials. Even in library school, we can remember being taught "collection development" in terms of how we should choose materials for our collections. Yet a good collection development policy consists of two opposite but equally important steps: purchasing new materials and weeding out those works which are no longer relevant to the collection. Many librarians find weeding difficult. Most of us became librarians because we love books, and asking us to remove even one from the shelf can be painful. To help ease your discomfort and allow you to develop the best possible horror collection for your library, we will provide some guidelines and recommendations for enhancing your existing collection. But be warned, this enhancement will require you to look critically at your current offerings, identify new materials to add, and, most importantly, designate books to discard. Hopefully, this chapter will provide some analgesic relief when it comes time to delete your weeded books' records from the catalog.

The first step in your horror collection development plan is to assess your current holdings in the genre. This may sound like a fairly easy task, but if you do not have experience with horror works, it can be a daunting exercise. Hopefully, any anxiety about your horror collection will be alleviated by the familiarity of our first recommended step. Simply begin your assessment by turning to the same print resources you already turn to for your general collection development—the review journals. For horror, you will have the most luck with the last few years' October issues. Specifically, *Booklist* chooses a guest editor each October to comment on the ten best horror novels of the past year. We suggest pulling at least the last three years' issues and checking your catalog against these lists. By seeing how many of the "best" horror works you have already acquired, you will get a quick sense of the relevance of your current collection. If you have many of these books, you will know that you have been doing a fairly good job picking up the newest horror fiction. On the other hand, if you find only a few of these works on your shelves, you may have quite a bit of work ahead of you. Depending on the popularity of horror at your library, we suggest filling in the gaps between your shelves and the last three years' lists as an easy way to quickly upgrade your horror collection with some solid works. You should also repeat this process with the last few years' award winners. (See chapter 14 for details.)

While it is important to have a good selection of the newest works on your shelves, be sure not to forget the best of the rest. Horror, like science fiction and fantasy, is a genre that is constantly paying homage to its history. Currently popular authors such as Stephen King, Neil Gaiman, and John Saul slip references to seminal works of horror into many of their novels and stories. Thus, after you complete the assessment of your current horror holdings, you need to turn to a few sources that list important older works. Chapter 14 in this book gives recommendations on sources to help you identify the "must have" older works, and if you need a quick yet thorough list you can turn to the Horror Writers Association's list of "The Best Horror Novels of All Time" at www.horror.org/readlist.htm. Check your holdings against this and other lists to make sure your shelves have a good selection of these seminal works of the macabre.

Now that you have quickly taken the pulse of your horror collection by checking your holdings against some key lists and by adding those works which were missed the first time around, it is time to begin weeding. Besides the fact that we all love books too much to pull them off the shelf forever, librarians also find weeding difficult because unlike acquiring materials, there are no "reviews" or published lists of works recommended for weeding. Weeding guidelines must be developed at the local level. Each library will have its own guidelines dictating what materials should be removed from the collection, and those parameters will almost certainly be different for each genre. The only certainty in weeding is that it will be a physically and emotionally exhausting exercise, but at the end of your labors, you will have created the most effective collection for your patrons.

You should not begin the weeding process without establishing general guidelines. We will recommend some ideas and processes that have worked for us and our horror collection, but each library needs to take the time to consider its entire collection and its patrons before deleting records by the dozen. With that word of caution, we suggest that you begin by assessing the condition of your books. Pull everything that is tattered, ripped, shabby, or has a generic bindery cover, and look critically at these worn materials. Using your predetermined weeding guidelines, decide which works you will delete and write down the titles and authors of those you wish to keep. Now get rid of all of those worn books, and only order new copies of the titles you have decided to keep. We have found that books which are in bad physical condition do not get read. So use the beginning of your weeding process as an excuse to finally replace that tattered copy of *The Shining*.

Now comes the time to tackle the bulk of the collection. The next parameter for identifying candidates for removal is by checking each work's circulation record. Generally, if the work is rarely—or never—read and is not found in *The Fiction Catalog* or *Hooked on Horror,* you can safely get rid of it. Even if a book won a Bram Stoker Award seven years ago, if no one at your library has ever read it, you can safely assume it will continue to stay put on the shelf. You also need to look critically at your older horror novels to make sure they are still relevant to your current readers. With today's graphic splatterpunk and sexually explicit vampire novels, many older works of horror appear downright hokey to the younger reader. Just be careful not to weed out a seminal or groundbreaking work along the way. These suggestions should get you started, but in order to create the correct weeding plan for your library, you must take the time to learn about the collection you are trying to thin and the readers who will be affected by your decisions.

Any good weeding plan should bring you right back to the acquisition side of collection development. As you weed the collection it will become obvious where your horror holdings are lacking. Your newly streamlined horror collection, trimmed of irrelevant and unread works and newly beefed up with the best of the newer works and fresh, crisp copies of the all-time greats, is ripe for a visit from some of your most avid horror readers. We suggest coupling one of your horror programs with a discussion of your patrons' horror reading habits. Invite interested readers to be part of an informal advisory group. These patrons are your local horror experts; they are the ones reading what you are buying, so why not include them in the process? This advisory group can be comprised of as many or as few patrons as you want. For example, when we took over the readers' advisory desk at the Berwyn Public Library, our fantasy collection was a mess. Although the books were checked out quite often, the collection was too large and was extremely out-of-date. As part of our process to create a more efficient fantasy collection, we employed one of our most avid and widely read fantasy patrons. He let us know where the gaps in our collection were, pointed out works that could be tossed, and even looked over the reviews of current fantasy materials to make purchasing suggestions to us. While we did not blindly follow all of his recommendations, this patron's input was a helpful piece of our collection development puzzle. If creating some kind of "horror advisory board" would not work at your library, you could go to the experts yourself by taking a field trip to the nearest occult bookstore. Establishing a relationship with the owner and staff gives you access to horror aficionados for all of your collection development questions.

Unfortunately, even after working to assess your horror holdings, acquire new materials, and weed out the irrelevant works, your job is far from done. An effective collection development policy is constantly in use. You need to stay up-to-date on all of the new horror offerings being published. You can turn to chapter 14 for suggestions on how to stay informed. There are also a number of publishers, both large and small, who specialize in horror. Figure 15-1 lists a few of these, but a complete list of publishers with links to each of their home pages can be found on the Horror Writers Association's website at www.horror.org/horrorlinks. htm. Finally, you will need to revisit your horror collection for assessment and weeding every three to five years, depending on the size and circulation statistics of your collection. Ideally, you are following the collection development guidelines found in this chapter for each of your genres. This means you are constantly weeding, attacking a new genre each year. We know firsthand how hard it is to create and implement a useful collection deployment policy. The process can be labor-intensive and overwhelming at times, but the hardest part is tackling a neglected genre the first time. Once you get things in order, the maintenance is not only easy; it can also be fun.

Major Publishers	*Small Press Publishers*
Arkham House	Dark Highway Press
Baen Books	Delirium Books
Chaosium	Donald M. Grant, Publisher
DAW Books	Edgewood Press
Del Rey Books	Four Walls-Eight Windows
Penguin	Garcia Publishing Services/
Tor Books	American Fantasy Press
White Wolf	Gauntlet Press
	Lone Wolf Publications
	Meisha Merlin Publishing
	Necronomicon Press
	Wildside Press

FIGURE 15-1   Horror Publishers

16

Marketing Your Horror Collection

*Make Them Come Back
to Your Lair of Horror*

Marketing is not just for business school graduates anymore. Librarians are beginning to use business and marketing techniques with more savvy. With the proliferation of Barnes and Noble and Borders bookstores and with competition from Amazon.com, public libraries have to work harder now to remind people that they can have all the books they want for *free* at their local library. Marketing campaigns in public libraries must be forged on two fronts, however. Librarians must grab the community's interest and bring people into the library, and then they can highlight their collections once the patrons have come through the door. And horror fiction may need an even more aggressive marketing campaign than other genres. Since it is the rare library that pulls horror out of the main fiction collection and gives the genre its own section, the readers' advisor must find methods for singling horror out from the larger section in which it is embedded. Effective horror marketing will also give you credibility with die-hard horror readers. Once these patrons feel you have a grasp of the genre they love, we have found that they tend to open up, asking you for assistance with locating materials and sharing their vast knowledge with you.

Unfortunately, most libraries only market their horror collections during the month of October. Since you already have a Halloween-primed audience, and every library resource from *Booklist* to NoveList provides dozens of display ideas and booklists, October really is the easiest time of year to highlight your horror offerings. However, you cannot fully capitalize on this interest without highlighting horror at other times of the year as well. One month may provide enough time for your patrons to check out a couple of books from your Halloween display. But where is that display three weeks later when they return the books? Marketing is about letting patrons know what they would love to read, if only they knew about it beforehand. The patron who discovers a love for horror in October may not know where to find more. In order to solve this dilemma, we will lay out some ideas and methods to help you to make your horror collection shine during any season.

October: File and Save

The key to successful horror fiction marketing begins in October. It is hard to avoid horror marketing ideas during the Halloween season, so take advantage of it. Clip and print every idea you come across. Check all of the monthly library publications and websites. Also, don't forget commercial websites like Amazon.com and BN.com (Barnes and Noble); they always print a list of horror books in October. Your library is probably also planning some sort of horror-related programming to coincide with Halloween. Talk to whoever plans programs (if it is you, even better), and ask for information on the upcoming program and any other programs they are considering for that time. Now you have a huge pile of papers cluttering your work area. Step one is to "file." Take all of these clippings and put them into a folder marked "Horror." Do not label it "Halloween." Although you generated the information because of Halloween, this does not mean you are obligated to use it only during the month of October. Labeling the file "Horror" will also make it easier to locate these valuable resources when horror-related questions arise during the other eleven months of the year. Use what you need to help you make your displays and booklists for Halloween (remembering to place copies of what you did in the folder), and move on to step two, "save." Use this folder to save most of the ideas for the future because, as we will outline in this chapter, there are plenty of opportunities throughout the year to place the spotlight on horror.

Getting the Word Out in the Community

While most people know they can go to their library for the latest Stephen King offering, many fail to realize how much more their public library has to offer when it comes to horror. Therefore, before you can worry about how to market the horror fiction you have to current patrons, you must first spread the word about your horror offerings to the community at large. While this type of target marketing can work for any genre or service that the library wants to emphasize, we will focus on how it can work best for horror. By having horror-related programming, utilizing your library's website, and going out into the community yourself, you can both identify those interested in horror and possibly create new fans for the genre.

Libraries seem to be most comfortable with marketing themselves through the "edutainment" programs they offer to the community. Programming, especially adult programming, is the easiest way to draw people's attention and bring them into the library. Since we are dealing with horror, you will want to create programming for patrons from approximately age fifteen and up. If you have never organized a program, or you feel you are fresh out of ideas, we recommend looking at one of the latest books in the American Library Association's series on programming, Brett Lear's *Adult Programs in the Library.*[1] This guide will provide you with plenty of advice on how to put on the perfect adult program, no matter what your topic.

While Lear's book outlines the basics of general adult programming, in order to specifically target your programs to the horror-loving audience, we have a couple of proven suggestions. The easiest way to get ideas is to call other libraries in your area and ask them what they have done for Halloweens past. Take down the names of any performers who were a hit for them, and make sure to share anything that has worked at your library too. But your best bet for ideas will undoubtedly come from your local historical society. Every town, county, or at least every state has a "haunted history." Whether you are dealing with legends, ghost stories, or even just the graves of famous people, there is "true" horror to be found in your local history. Talk to the local historians and look for any books published about haunted happenings in your area. If you ask them, these historians, or maybe even an author, might be willing to come give a talk at the library. We have found that horror tends to generate its largest audience when it is linked to "true" events. For example, here in northeastern Illinois we have a very popular book entitled *Chicago Haunts: Ghostly Lore of the Windy City* by Ursula Bielski.[2] This is one of the most frequently stolen books at our library. Since our patrons love to delve into the supernatural past of the Chicagoland area, we try to offer them horror programming that is linked to their community.

Once you have done all the brainstorming, planning, and booking for your program, don't forget that the key to successful programming of any kind is in the advertising. We know this is yet another business world term, but unfortunately, the library is only one of many places where the community can turn for recreation, and you won't be able to compete without making an effort to advertise your exciting offerings. Start with the press. Because you are a public library, the local papers will run press releases about your upcoming programs at no charge. Also, don't forget the power of making an eye-catching flyer. We recommend taking a class or attending a seminar on creating flyers and pamphlets. Our flyers became much more effective after Tammy did this. We include here an example of a flyer from a Halloween program we presented on "Vampires" in 2001. (See figure 16-1.) We have also found that purchasing a decent graphics software program makes the entire advertising process go more smoothly. Print Shop is one we use. It is inexpensive and it comes with plenty of horror-related graphics. After you have made a beautiful flyer of your own, make sure it gets distributed throughout the community. Besides your usual drop-off spots, for horror programs, try to have flyers put up at local high schools and any comic book shops in your area. With this much planning, your horror program is sure to be a success!

While horror programs are going to be infrequent and eat up a lot of time and money, your library's website is a cheap way to advertise your horror collection all year round. Surfing the website may not give your patrons full access to all of your services, but you can use it to provide enough information to entice them into coming in to check out the real thing for themselves. In order to ensure success in marketing horror on your site, make sure you have first set aside a portion of the site for all fiction and fiction services. Then feature a different fiction genre each month. Of course, horror will probably get the focus in October, but that is fine because due to the nature of the Web, once you are done highlighting horror it does not have to go away completely. Within the "Fiction" section of your website, create a subsection for the different genres, each filled with booklists by subgenre, highlights on new authors, or simply annotations for some of your favorite books. (See figures 16-2A to 16-2D.) Also, include some links to other web-based sources. (See chapter 14.) Each month you can simply update the information for the chosen genre, in this

In time for Halloween, the Berwyn Public Library Presents . . .

Vampires: Creatures of the Night

Join us for a slide presentation by Martin V. Riccardo, as he explains the mysteries of the vampire in legend, film, fantasy, and fact. Many aspects of the undead are covered, including: the origin and history of vampire beliefs, ancient lore of blood and the restless dead, and the attraction of the vampire in literature, movies, and culture.

SATURDAY, OCTOBER 27, 2001 2:00 P.M. COMMUNITY ROOM

PLEASE CALL FOR RESERVATIONS (708) 795-8000 EXT. 3005

Berwyn Public Library
2701 S. Harlem Ave.
Berwyn, IL 60402
(708) 795-8000 ext. 3005

FIGURE 16-1   Berwyn Public Library Flyer for a Halloween Program

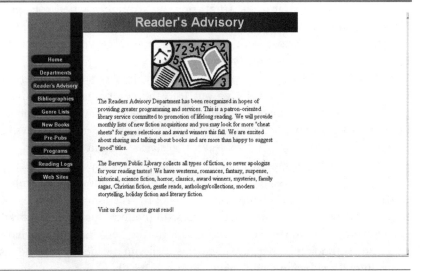

FIGURE 16-2A   Main Readers' Advisory Page on the Berwyn Public
Library's website, http://www.berwynlibrary.net/
Departments/Reader_ s_Advisory/reader_s_advisory.
html

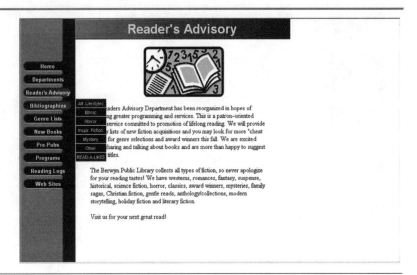

FIGURE 16-2B   Java Script Pop-up List Which Allows the User to Choose
a Specific Category of Bibliographies

case horror, and move it to the front page. In November, when you spotlight something else, you simply move the horror link to the bottom or side of the "Fiction" page with your other genres. Now your patrons can use the website to access horror information all year long.

There is one final step the public librarian can take in order to get the word out—you can physically go out into the community and actively promote your collections and services. People have many entertainment options vying for their attention, so in order to remind them about the library's offerings, you need to leave the stacks behind and go to the patrons. Horror happens to provide a great opportunity for such active marketing. Adolescents are one of the largest demographic groups interested in horror; they also happen to be one of the easiest to reach because they can all be found in one place. Work with the local high school librarian to arrange for you to come and give a horror book talk. If you have never done a book talk, here are a few tips. Pick out a wide range of books from different subgenres and make sure to bring them with you. Spend less than five minutes describing the plot and appeal factors of each book. Try to make your descriptions interesting and suspenseful, and especially

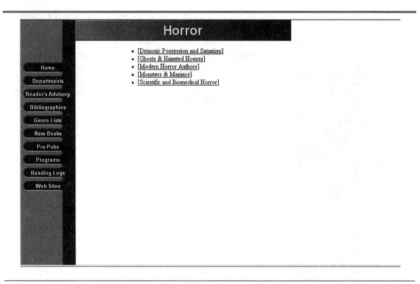

FIGURE 16-2C   Page the User Is Brought to After Choosing "Horror" from the Main Screen

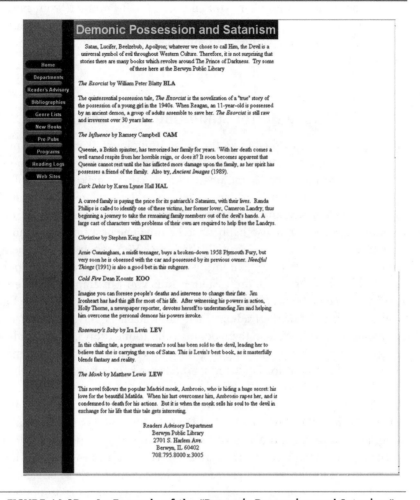

FIGURE 16-2D   An Example of the "Demonic Possession and Satanism" Bibliography As Found on the Website

with horror, do not give away the plot twists or endings. Once you finish with the first book, pass it around and let the kids handle it before you move on to the next title. Booktalking is a skill that you can never get wrong once learned; you will simply get more comfortable each time you try it. Finally, no matter where you end up going to promote your horror collection or how you do it, only good things can happen to the librarian who is brave enough to venture out into the community to promote his or her collections.

Making Horror Stand Out in the Stacks

Now that you have worked to let the community know that the local public library is a great place to come for their horror fiction, you have to put even more effort into the second phase of marketing—making your collection shine. Whether you work at the reference desk or are lucky enough to have a readers' advisory department, promoting different genres is time-consuming; however, it also happens to be fun. The best thing you can do to market your fiction is to read all the time. Who can argue with being paid to read? Besides having an intimate relationship with as many books as possible, there are some professional skills you can employ in order to highlight specific books or genres. Joyce Saricks and Nancy Brown lay out many of the tricks of the trade in their book *Readers' Advisory Service in the Public Library*.[3] We use their book as the foundation for our readers' advisory service, so instead of going through each of their recommendations, we will instead focus on the methods we have successfully utilized in marketing our horror collection.

The best way to expose interested patrons to other horror books is to get them while they are on the hold list for a horror best seller. Stephen King, Dean Koontz, and Anne Rice are three of the most popular authors in the country. Each time they publish a book, libraries generate long reserve lists. But why should patrons who have come for these books have to go home empty-handed? Each hold your library places is an opportunity to promote your other worthy horror offerings. The simplest way to accomplish this is to make bookmarks listing "Read-a-Likes" for the current best seller. Anne Rice books are the easiest because most of her novels deal with vampires. You can create a bookmark for her like the one shown in figure 16-3 and print them each time she publishes a new vampire book. Leave them on your desk in a prominent area and have them available to be handed out each time someone places a hold on her book. King and Koontz are a bit more tricky; you will have to tailor your bookmark lists to each book, because both authors tend not only to cross into different horror subgenres, but are also known to move into completely different genres. Read the reviews of their newest offerings and try to create a list of Read-a-Likes from this information. We actually recommend *against* putting yourself at the top of the reserve list so you can read the book first. The small advantage you get from being intimately familiar with the book is greatly outweighed by the inconvenience you have caused your patrons by delaying their chance to read their favorite author's newest book.

Creating these bookmarks and aggressively handing them out gives your patrons another reading option while they wait, and it also exposes readers who have already shown an interest in horror novels to other works in the genre. While we find this marketing technique to be very useful, especially with these three authors, we do have a word of caution. Do not get discouraged if people refuse your advances, because they will. We are very proactive in our promotion (we actually go after patrons much like a salesperson does at the store), and we still frequently find that many patrons only use the library to read their favorite authors. Even with well-designed prodding, some people will not venture

Don't just hang around waiting for the new Anne Rice, try one of these vampire tales while you wait . . .

Lost Souls by Poppy Z. Brite—**BRI**

Sunglasses after Dark by Nancy Collins—**COL**

Those Who Hunt the Night by Barbara Hambly—**HAM**

Obsidian Butterfly by Laurell Hamilton—**HAM**

Children of the Vampire by Jeanne Kalogridis—**KAL**

Salem's Lot by Stephen King—**KIN**

Anno Dracula by Kim Newman—**NEW**

Dracula by Bram Stoker—**STO**

The Soul of an Angel by Chelsea Quinn Yarbro—**YAR**

. . . And don't forget to ask your helpful Readers' Advisor for more great reading suggestions.

FIGURE 16-3 Sample Bookmark

away from the familiar. So look at each patron you can match up with another horror book as its own success story.

Your next promotion option is the tried-and-true display, but we always add a few twists to this common marketing technique. Anyone can pull horror books off the shelf and put them on display, but we spice it up by always accompanying the display with an annotated list of the corresponding books. This display can be done at Halloween, but let us give you another example of a successful horror-themed display. Horror movies come out in the theaters throughout the year, and most of them are either based on a book or written by a known horror author (Stephen King and Clive Barker's books are often made into films). This creates the perfect opportunity to not only display the book upon which the movie is based, but to also include other books from that subgenre. For instance, in 1999 *The Haunting* with Liam Neeson and Catherine Zeta-Jones was released. This movie was based on the classic Shirley Jackson novel *The Haunting of Hill House.* You could use the opportunity which popular culture has thrust upon you and display all of your haunted house and ghost stories in conjunction with the film's release. Then, once you have the books out, make up an annotated list of all of the books you own in this subgenre, place it next to the display, and upload a copy to your website (don't forget to file a copy in the "Horror" folder we had you create earlier). We have also found it helpful to always include the call numbers for the books you are listing. This makes it easier for you and your patrons to find the materials when they are not on display. Once you have it all set up, interested patrons will browse the display area, but more importantly, they have a list of similar horror books which they can refer to long after the display is taken down.

As we mentioned before, most libraries do not have the space to pull out horror into its own section. Some libraries group it with fantasy, and others, like our library, unfortunately, have it mixed in with the general fiction. Because horror, like other embedded genres, is hard to locate in the stacks, we make a point to occasionally "flag" our horror books. We do the same thing with Oprah books, "inspirational fiction," and westerns, which are all filed within the general fiction, but *we only flag one of these genres at a time.* What do we mean by flag? Well, this leads us to reveal our biggest marketing secret. Everything you print in your efforts to promote horror should be done on the same colored paper. For example, we use purple for Oprah books, hot pink for inspirational fiction, green for westerns and, of course, orange for horror. Every bookmark, sign, display, and flyer that we produce in an effort to market horror is done on the same orange paper. This consistency has allowed our patrons to associate a specific color with a particular genre. This brings us back to the flags. Once you have trained your patrons to match a color with a genre, you can place bookmark-sized bibliographies on orange paper in your horror books. These flags will stick out of the books and allow your horror collection to rise out of the crowded stacks as well as suggest other possible titles. People who love horror will migrate toward the flagged books, and those who may have never considered the genre before will be intrigued enough by the bookmarks to at least take a look at a horror book.

While these suggestions for promoting horror fiction have worked at our library, there is no guarantee they will work at yours. Marketing of any kind must be tailored to the needs, desires, and interests of those in your community. Also, you may have even better ideas that we have yet to try. Just remember that the key to highlighting your horror books is to use what works. That may mean going through a period of trial and error, but once you find what works, stick with it! We try to live by this rule, and as a result, our patrons seem to enjoy the consistency we provide. For example, they now know that no matter what we are displaying there will be an annotated list, and they are always on the lookout for the new flags we have placed throughout the collection. The payoff for all your hard work comes a few months after you put together that wonderful horror display, when a patron comes in with a marked-up copy of the accompanying list and asks you to help him find one of the books. Trust us, if you do the work, it will happen.

Putting It All Together

Each of the marketing ideas we have laid out for you works well on its own; however, by putting them all together, you can be even more successful. When you book that program on vampires, make a date to go over to the high school to give a vampire-themed book talk two weeks before the program. Get your display (with annotated lists) up a good four weeks prior to the program and highlight the list on your home page. Finally, the day of the program, flag the horror books in the stacks. Then those patrons who are browsing after the program will be drawn to the other horror books in your collection. Although this type of marketing takes a great deal of preparation, give at least some of our ideas a try and see if they work for you. Whether it is October, April, or any month in between, we hope you give your horror books their much-deserved moment in the sun.

NOTES

1. Brett W. Lear, *Adult Programs in the Library* (Chicago: American Library Association, 2002).
2. Ursula Bielski, *Chicago Haunts: Ghostly Lore of the Windy City,* 2d ed. (Chicago: Lake Claremont, 1998). The success of this book has even spawned a sequel, *More Chicago Haunts: Scenes from Myth and Mystery* (Chicago: Lake Claremont, 2000). Bielski's books are only two among more than a dozen on haunted Chicago or Illinois history. Other states or regions will have many similar materials.
3. Joyce G. Saricks and Nancy Brown, *Readers' Advisory Service in the Public Library,* 2d ed. (Chicago: American Library Association, 1997). Although useful tips are found throughout the book, chapter 6 deals with promotion specifically.

The Big Three

Although there are many worthy horror writers, the genre is commercially dominated by three authors: Stephen King, Dean Koontz, and Anne Rice. We estimate that at least half of the horror-related questions and inquiries the average readers' advisor receives will have to do with one of these three authors. Therefore, we have designed this appendix to be used as a ready reference resource for the most common of these questions. Here we provide basic information about each author, a few resources you or your patrons can turn to for more in-depth information, and most importantly, a list of each author's works in chronological order. We do not provide annotations in this section. This appendix is merely a resource to locate information on each author and to quickly look up a list of their works. However, many of these books are annotated in the regular chapters of this book. You can use the index to locate these.

Stephen King

No book could be written on horror fiction without placing the spotlight upon the genre's most popular author, Stephen King. In fact, few writers have had more impact upon the entire literary community over the last twenty-five years than King. The following are some statistics compiled by Michael Collings that illustrate this influence. King ranked second in the list of authors with the most best-selling titles between 1965 and 1985; Virginia Holt held the top spot with 10 titles in 11 years, while King had 9 (*The Shining* through *The Talisman*) in 9 years. During the 520 weeks from August 1976 through July 1986, King's name appeared on the best-seller lists at least 545 times, which made for an unprecedented average of 1.05

titles *per week* over a 10-year span. In 1981 King made publishing history when he had three titles on the best-seller list at the same time; and in 1985 he broke even this record. Stephen King has also made the best-seller list with novels, short story collections, and nonfiction—a very rare feat.[1]

As a horror writer King has no peer. He has written in every major subgenre and has been involved with bringing dozens of his works to the big screen. In 1981 King published a nonfiction work on horror itself entitled *Stephen King's Danse Macabre.*[2] Most readers are introduced to horror fiction through King; thus, it is important for the librarian to have at least a basic understanding of King's life and works. Luckily, this is an easy task because King has not been shy about making his life story public knowledge. Between his memoir and countless interviews, King has told the world of his poor childhood, broken home, teaching career, drug addiction, and his ultimate success. The two best sources for biographical information on King can be found in his 2000 memoir, *On Writing: A Memoir of the Craft,*[3] and his official website, at www.stephenking.com.[4]

In the last decade King has gained more respect as a serious author. This process began in earnest in 1996 when he won the O'Henry Award for his short story "The Man in the Black Suit." Harold Bloom has even included King in his acclaimed series of literary criticism.[5] In the fall of 2003 the National Book Foundation shocked the literary world by presenting King with its 2003 Distinguished Contribution to American Letters award. King is slowly but surely making the case for horror's place within the canon of modern literature, and the literary community is beginning to listen.

Bibliography (Fiction Only)

Carrie. 1974.

Salem's Lot. 1975.

The Shining. 1977.

The Night Shift. 1978.

The Stand. 1978. (Reprinted unabridged in 1990 with 150,000 additional words)

The Dead Zone. 1979.

Cujo. 1981.

Firestarter. 1981.

Creepshow. 1982.

The Dark Tower: The Gunslinger. 1982.

Different Seasons. 1982.

Christine. 1983.

Cycle of the Werewolf. 1983.

Pet Sematary. 1983.

The Talisman. 1984.

Skeleton Crew. 1985.

It. 1986.

The Dark Tower II: The Drawing of the Three. 1987.

The Eyes of the Dragon. 1987.

The Tommyknockers. 1987.

The Dark Tower III: The Waste Lands. 1988.

Misery. 1988.

The Dark Half. 1989.

Four Past Midnight. 1990.

Needful Things. 1991.

Dolores Claiborne. 1992.

Gerald's Game. 1992.

Nightmares and Dreamscapes. 1993.

Insomnia. 1994.

Rose Madder. 1995.

Desperation. 1996.

The Green Mile. 1996.

The Dark Tower IV: Wizard and Glass. 1997.

Bag of Bones. 1998.

The Girl Who Loved Tom Gordon. 1999.

Hearts in Atlantis. 1999.

Storm of the Century. 1999.

The Plant. 2000–2001. (Electronic book; not completed)

The Black House. 2001.

Dreamcatcher. 2001.

Everything's Eventual: 14 Dark Tales. 2002.

From a Buick 8. 2002.

WRITING AS RICHARD BACHMAN

Rage. 1977.

The Long Walk. 1979.

Roadwork. 1981.

The Running Man. 1982.

Thinner. 1984.

The Regulators. 1996.

Dean Koontz

Good heavens, what's wrong with these people who don't like stories of the supernatural. —Dean Koontz, quoted in *The Dean Koontz Companion*

It has been noted that Dean Koontz is the "least-known best-selling author in America."[6] There could be many reasons for this. First, Koontz is fiercely private; he rarely gives interviews, and lives a quiet life with his wife in California. Koontz is also a workaholic; he writes eight to ten hours a day, every day. This work schedule leaves very little time to actively promote himself. What we do know about Koontz is that he is one of the most popular writers in America, and for that matter, one of our best pure storytellers. As David Silva noted, those stories that "tell the starkest truths—find a way of staying with you long after you finish their words. . . . Dean Koontz is a teller of stark truths."[7]

But is Koontz a horror writer? This is a question that has plagued all who have tried to pigeonhole the author. Koontz began his professional career in 1968 as a pure science fiction writer. He continued in this vein for four years, but began to feel constrained by the limits of the genre. In an attempt to branch out, Koontz began working in different genres (horror, suspense, techno-thrillers, romance, etc.). However, with each experiment Koontz used a different pen name. For the next fifteen years Koontz published numerous works under names like Deanna Dwyer, K. R. Dwyer, Brian Coffey, Anthony North, John Hill, Aaron Wolfe, David Axton, Leigh Nichols, Owen West, and Richard Paige. This trend finally ended in 1980 with Koontz's first cross-genre work, which also happened to be his first best seller, *Whispers*. In the twenty-plus ensuing years, Koontz has continued to blend genres in his work, yet when forced to classify him, people generally refer to him as a horror writer. Much of this has to do with his great skill in creating and sustaining fear throughout his works. This fear is so compelling because of its basis in reality, as Joan Kotker noted:

> Any discussion of Dean Koontz as a writer of horror fiction is inaccurate unless it emphasizes that in most of Koontz's work, horror is based on the inhumanity of one human being to another rather than on such stock supernatural devices as the cold, dismembered hand reaching out to touch someone, the door that mysteriously slams shut. . . . But there is nothing comforting about Dean Koontz's descriptions of the horrors we can and do inflict on each other, and it is for this reason that many of Dean Koontz's works stay in the mind long after they have been read: his fictional horrors can be all too real, and although he insists that we can overcome them, only some characters—the ones we identify with—ultimately succeed in doing so.[8]

It is this sense of unease with ourselves that Koontz has masterfully exploited in a long and profitable career.

For patrons who want more information about Koontz, we recommend two books. In 1994 Martin Greenberg, Ed Gorman, and Bill Munster published the best Koontz book available, *The Dean Koontz Companion*. This book is broken up into three distinct parts. The first contains a rare interview with Koontz, in which he discusses his personal life and feelings about his own work in great detail. He is quite frank about growing up poor in rural Pennsylvania, with a violently abusive father. This intriguing interview is followed by a group of essays about Koontz by other well-known horror writers, including David Silva and Charles de Lint. The last section of the book includes short original essays by Koontz himself in which he pontificates on life, his work, and the state of literature in general. For a more critical approach to Koontz's work, we recommend Joan Kotker's *Dean Koontz: A Critical Companion* (1996). Kotker begins with a great overview of Koontz and his work. She discusses his place among many genres and his road to success. Kotker then moves on to Koontz's major works and provides critical interpretations of these novels. The Greenberg work is best for the true Koontz fan, while the Kotker book is perfect for a student looking for a critical source.

Bibliography

Note: Dating Koontz's novels is a difficult undertaking. Many of his works were originally published under different pseudonyms and then republished later under his own name so publishers could get as much money as possible out of his subsequent fame. Also, some of his earlier novels are still in the process of being republished. As a result, we have compiled the best dated list of Koontz works that we could, using a combination of Fonseca and Pulliam's *Hooked on Horror,* Greenberg's book, and Koontz's publisher's website. In cases where sources contradicted each other, we relied on the publisher's website first and Greenberg second.

The Fall of the Dream Machine. 1969.

Fear That Man. 1969.

Anti-Man. 1970.

Beastchild. 1970.

Bounce Girl. 1970.

Dark of the Woods. 1970.

The Dark Symphony. 1970.

Hell's Gate. 1970.

Soft Come the Dragons. 1970.

The Crimson Witch. 1971.

A Darkness in My Soul. 1972.

The Flesh in the Furnace. 1972.

Starblood. 1972.

Time Thieves. 1972.

Warlock. 1972.

Demon Seed. 1973.

Hanging On. 1973.

The Haunted Earth. 1973.

Shattered. 1973.

A Werewolf among Us. 1973.

After the Last Race. 1974.

Nightmare Journey. 1975.

Night Chills. 1976.

Vision. 1977.

Whispers. 1980.

Phantoms. 1983.

The Darkfall. 1984.

The Face of Fear. 1985.

The Servants of Twilight. 1985.

Twilight Eyes. 1985.

Strangers. 1986.

Shadowfires. 1987.

Watchers. 1987.

The House of Thunder. 1988.

Lightning. 1988.

The Mask. 1988.

Oddkins. 1988.

The Eyes of Darkness. 1989.

The Key to Midnight. 1989.

Midnight. 1989.

The Bad Place. 1990.

Chase. 1991.

Cold Fire. 1991.

The Voice of the Night. 1991.

Hideaway. 1992.

Dragon Tears. 1993.

Mr. Murder. 1993.

Dark Rivers of the Heart. 1994.

The Door to December. 1994.

Fun House. 1994.

Winter Moon. 1994.

Ice Bound. 1995.

Intensity. 1995.

Strange Highways. 1995.

Santa's Twin. 1996.

Sole Survivor. 1996.

Ticktock. 1996.

The Vision. 1997.

Fear Nothing. 1998.

False Memory. 1999.

Seize the Night. 1999.

From the Corner of His Eye. 2001.

One Door Away from Heaven. 2001.

By the Light of the Moon. 2002.

Anne Rice

Since the publication of her first book, *Interview with the Vampire,* in 1976, Anne Rice has both mastered and transcended the familiar vampire genre. No other author since Bram Stoker has affected how we view these supernatural creatures more as she delves into the themes of good versus evil and morality and immorality in her epic fantasies. Because Rice identifies with the vampire rather than his victims, she "brings a fresh and powerful imagination to the staples of vampire lore; she makes well-known coffins and crucifixes tell new tales that compose a chilling original myth," observed Nina Auerbach in the *New York Times Book Review.*[9] Her beautiful, tortured characters are all too human; trapped in immortality, they suffer human emotions of loneliness, self doubt, sexual ambiguity, and guilt.

Anne Rice writes dark and sensuous stories. Walter Kendricks, of the *Voice Literary Supplement,* succinctly summarized the author's wide appeal and success by saying, "Rice's most effective accomplishment . . . was to link up sex and fear again."[10] In her novels she has pushed the boundaries of our most deeply held cultural assumptions about what is evil and on human sexuality in its many forms. Ferociously criticized, Rice unapologetically allows her flawed antiheroes to express their erotic natures in a decadent fashion. Taking this exploration of sexuality a step further, she has written highly erotic non-monster novels under the pseudonym Anne Rampling, and pure erotica under the name A. N. Roquelaure.

Through interviews, online discussions, tours of her New Orleans antebellum home, and semiautobiographical characters within her novels, Rice has allowed her fans a glance into her personal life. She has told of the death of her daughter, her own near death from diabetes, her marriage to the poet and artist Stan Rice, and her surprise at learning that her son Christopher, an author himself, was gay. Several books have been written about her and the characters in her novels. For more biographical information, take a look at *Conversations with Anne Rice: An Intimate, Enlightening Portrait of Her Life and Work,* by Michael Riley and Anne Rice; *The Gothic World of Anne Rice,* edited by Gary Hoppenstand and Ray B. Browne; *Anne Rice,* by Bette B. Roberts; *Anne Rice: A Critical Companion,* by Jennifer Smith; and Rice's official website at http://www.annerice.com.

Bibliography

CHRONICLES OF THE VAMPIRES

Interview with the Vampire. 1976.

The Vampire Lestat. 1985.

The Queen of the Damned. 1988.

The Tale of the Body Thief. 1992.

Memnoch the Devil. 1995.

The Vampire Armand. 1998.

Merrick. 2000.

Blood and Gold. 2001.

NEW TALES OF THE VAMPIRES

Pandora. 1998.

Vittorio, the Vampire. 1999.

MAYFAIR WITCHES

The Witching Hour. 1990.

Lasher. 1993.

Taltos. 1994.

MUMMY

The Mummy, or Ramses the Damned. 1989.

GHOST/SPIRIT/GENIE

Servant of the Bones. 1996.

Violin. 1997.

SHORT STORIES

The Master of Rampling Gate.
2002. (Audio format)

WRITING AS ANNE RAMPLING

Exit to Eden. 1985.

Belinda. 1986.

WRITING AS A. N. ROQUELAURE

The Charming of Sleeping Beauty.
1983.

Beauty's Punishment. 1984.

Beauty's Release. 1985.

NOTES

1. Michael R. Collings, *Scaring Us to Death: The Impact of Stephen King on Popular Culture,* The Milford Series: Popular Writers of Today 63 (San Bernadino, Calif.: Borgo, 1997), 44–47.
2. Stephen King, *Stephen King's Danse Macabre* (New York: Everest House, 1981).
3. Stephen King, *On Writing: A Memoir of the Craft* (New York: Scribner, 2000).
4. King's website is among the best we have ever encountered for an author. He has a complete bibliography of everything he has ever written and a fairly complete compilation of everything ever written about him.
5. Harold Bloom, ed., *Modern Critical Views: Stephen King* (Philadelphia: Chelsea House, 1998).
6. Karen Springen as quoted in Joan G. Kotker, *Dean Koontz: A Critical Companion* (Westport, Conn.: Greenwood, 1996), 9.
7. David Silva, "Keeping Pace with the Master," in *The Dean Koontz Companion,* by Martin Greenberg, Ed Gorman, and Bill Munster (New York: Berkley, 1994), 59.
8. Kotker, *Dean Koontz,* 14–15.
9. *Contemporary Authors, New Revision Series* (Detroit: Gale, 2002), 100:377.

BIBLIOGRAPHY

This bibliography provides a list of all the sources consulted for this book. For a detailed description of sources that are especially useful, see chapter 14, "Horror Resources."

Horror References

Ashley, Mike. *Who's Who in Horror and Fantasy Fiction*. New York: Taplinger, 1977.

Barclay, Glen St. John. *Anatomy of Horror: The Masters of Occult Fiction*. New York: St. Martin's, 1978.

Barron, Neil, ed. *Horror Literature: A Reader's Guide*. New York: Garland, 1990.

———. *Fantasy and Horror: A Critical and Historical Guide to Literature, Illustration, Film, TV, Radio, and the Internet*. Lanham, Md.: Scarecrow, 1999.

Bielski, Ursula. *Chicago Haunts: Ghostly Lore of the Windy City*. 2d ed. Chicago: Lake Claremont, 1998.

———. *More Chicago Haunts: Scenes from Myth and Mystery*. Chicago: Lake Claremont, 2000.

Bloom, Harold, ed. *Modern Critical Views: Stephen King*. Philadelphia: Chelsea House, 1998.

Burgess, Michael. *Reference Guide to Science Fiction, Fantasy, and Horror*. Englewood, Colo.: Libraries Unlimited, 1992.

Carter, Margaret L. "A Gravedigger's Dozen of Outstanding Vampire Tales." http://www.simegen.com/reviews/vampires/gravedig.htm.

Clark, Donia. "From Dracula to Hannibal: Escaping into Horror." *ILA Reporter* 10, no. 4 (August 2002): 10–11.

Collings, Michael R. *Scaring Us to Death: The Impact of Stephen King on Popular Culture.* The Milford Series: Popular Writers of Today 63. San Bernardino, Calif.: Borgo, 1997.

DarkEcho (online horror magazine). http://www.darkecho.com.

Datlow, Ellen, and Terry Windling. *The Year's Best Fantasy and Horror.* 13th annual collection. New York: St. Martin's, 2000.

Douglas, Drake. *Horror!* New York: Macmillan, 1966.

Everson, William. *Classics of the Horror Film.* New York: Citadel, 1990.

Fonseca, Anthony J., and June Michele Pulliam. *Hooked on Horror: A Guide to Reading Interests in Horror Fiction.* Englewood, Colo.: Libraries Unlimited, 1999. 2d ed., 2003.

Frank, Alan G. *The Movie Treasury: Horror Movies: Tales of Terror in the Cinema.* London: Octopus, 1974.

Frank, Frederick S. *Through the Pale Door: A Guide to and through the American Gothic.* New York: Greenwood, 1990.

Gifford, Denis. *A Pictorial History of Horror Movies.* New York: Hamlyn, 1973.

Golden, Christopher. *Cut!: Horror Writers on Horror Films.* New York: Berkley, 1992.

Gothic.Net (online horror magazine). http://www.gothic.net.

Greenberg, Martin, Ed Gorman, and Bill Munster. *The Dean Koontz Companion.* New York: Berkley, 1994.

Heller, Terry. *The Delights of Terror: An Aesthetics of the Tale of Terror.* Chicago: University of Illinois Press, 1987.

Horror Writers Association. http://www.horror.org.

Hutchinson, Tom, and Roy Pickard. *Horror: A History of Horror Movies.* Secaucus, N.J.: Chartwell, 1984.

International Horror Guild. http://www.ihgonline.org.

Jones, Stephen, ed. *Clive Barker's A–Z of Horror.* New York: Carroll and Graf, 1998.

Jones, Stephen, and Kim Newman, eds. *Horror: The Best 100 Books.* New York: Carroll and Graf, 1998.

King, Stephen. *Stephen King's Danse Macabre*. New York: Everest House, 1981.

———. *On Writing: A Memoir of the Craft*. New York: Scribner, 2000.

Kotker, Joan G. *Dean Koontz: A Critical Companion*. Westport, Conn.: Greenwood, 1996.

Newsom, Ted, director. *100 Years of Horror*. 2 videocassettes. North Hollywood, Calif.: Passport Video, 1996.

———. *100 Years of Horror*. 5 videocassettes. North Hollywood, Calif.: Passport Video, 1996.

Perry, Janet, and Victor Gentle. *Zombies*. Milwaukee, Wis.: Gareth Stevens, 1999.

Poe, Edgar Allan. *The Complete Tales and Poems of Edgar Allan Poe*. New York: Modern Library, 1938.

Pringle, David, ed. *St. James Guide to Horror, Ghost and Gothic Writers*. Detroit: St. James/Gale, 1998.

Punter, David. *The Literature of Terror: A History of Gothic Fictions from 1765 to the Present Day*. 2d ed. Vol. 1, *The Gothic Tradition*. New York: Longman, 1996.

Richardson, Beverley. "Changing Trends in Vampire Fiction." http://www.chebucto.ns.ca/~vampire/fictrend.html.

Shocklines: Your One-Stop Shop for Horror. http://www.shop.store.yahoo.com/shocklines.

Skal, David J. *The Monster Show: A Cultural History of Horror*. New York: W. W. Norton, 1993.

Stacy, Jan, and Ryder Syvertsen. *The Great Book of Movie Monsters*. Chicago: Contemporary, 1983.

Stealth Press Online. http://www.stealthpress.com.

Stuprich, Michael, ed. *The Greenhaven Press Companion to Literary Movements and Genres: Horror*. San Diego, Calif.: Greenhaven, 2001.

Time-Life Books, eds. *Transformations*. Alexandria, Va.: Time-Life, 1989.

Twitchell, James. *Dreadful Pleasures: An Anatomy of Modern Horror*. New York: Oxford University Press, 1985.

Tymn, Marshall B., ed. *Horror Literature: A Core Collection and Reference Guide*. New York: R. R. Bowker, 1981.

Vampire Book Bibliography. http://www.afn.org/~vampires/bkslist.html.

Weird Tales: The Unique Magazine. Official website. http://www. weird-tales.com/index.html.

Winter, Douglas E., ed. *Prime Evil: New Stories by the Masters of Modern Horror.* New York: New American Library, 1988.

Wordwalker (screen name). "These Are a Few of My Favorite Fangs." *Epinions.* http://www.epinions.com/book-review-7C3E-40FA618-39A3205E-prod4.

General References

a.k.a.: author pseudonyms, aliases, nicknames, working names, legalized names, pen names, noms des plumes, maiden names . . . etc. http://www.trussel.com/books/pseudo.htm.

Amazon.com. http://www.amazon.com.

Barnes and Noble Online. http://www.bn.com.

Booklist. Chicago: American Library Association. Also available online at http://www.ala.org/booklist.

Books in Print Plus (subscription service). R. R. Bowker. (http://booksinprint.com.

Fiction-L (electronic discussion list). http://www.webrary.org/rs/FLmenu.html.

Herald, Diana Tixier. *Genreflecting: A Guide to Reading Interests in Genre Fiction.* 5th ed. Englewood, Colo.: Libraries Unlimited, 2000.

Lear, Brett W. *Adult Programs in the Library.* Chicago: American Library Association, 2002.

Lesher, Linda Parent. *The Best Novels of the Nineties: A Reader's Guide.* Jefferson, N.C.: McFarland, 2000.

NoveList (subscription service). EBSCO Publishing. http://search.epnet.com.

Saricks, Joyce G. *The Readers' Advisory Guide to Genre Fiction.* Chicago: American Library Association, 2001.

Saricks, Joyce G., and Nancy Brown. *Readers' Advisory Service in the Public Library.* 2d ed. Chicago: American Library Association, 1997.

System Wide Automated Network (SWAN). Burr Ridge, Ill.: Suburban Library System Catalog. http://swan.sls.lib.il.us/.

Title Source II (subscription service). Baker and Taylor. http://ts2b.informata.com/TS2/.

Yaakov, Juliette, and John Greenfield. *The Fiction Catalog*. 14th ed. New York: H. W. Wilson, 2001.

INDEX

Authors, editors, titles, subjects, and series are interfiled in one alphabet. Author names appear in roman type, book titles in italics, and subjects in boldface. Series and short stories are in quotation marks.

Becky Siegel Spratford is a Readers' Advisory librarian at the Berwyn Public Library in Berwyn, Illinois. She co-created the Readers' Advisory Department there in 2000. Spratford provides readers' advisory help to patrons and selects fiction. She received her M.L.I.S. degree with honors from Dominican University in 2001.

Tammy Hennigh Clausen is a public librarian and manager of the Readers' Advisory Department at the Berwyn Public Library just west of Chicago. She moved from New Mexico to attend Dominican University, graduating with an M.L.I.S. degree in 2002. She was formerly the Adult Services librarian at the Cicero Public Library. Working in public libraries for more than ten years, Clausen eventually found her niche at the Berwyn Public Library.